D1741225

THE
MARKETING
EDGE

THE MARKETING EDGE

Key to Profit and Growth

TONY McBURNIE

AND

DAVID CLUTTERBUCK

Weidenfeld and Nicolson
London

First published in Great Britain in 1987 by
George Weidenfeld & Nicolson Limited
91 Clapham High Street, London SW4 7TA

Copyright © 1987 The Winning Streak Limited and Tony McBurnie

All rights reserved. No part of this publication may
be reproduced, stored in a retrieval system, or
transmitted in any form or by any means, electronic,
mechanical, photocopying, recording or otherwise,
without the prior permission of the copyright owner.

ISBN 0 297 78985 6

Printed in Great Britain by The Bath Press, Avon

Contents

CONTENTS

Introduction

It is a universal truism that there is no business until a customer actually buys your product or service. Yet for all the lipservice companies give to being market oriented, it is remarkable how few of them have really taken on board the full implications of that simple statement. The plain fact is that if even half the major (let alone the minor) companies in Britain understood and reacted to customers' needs as well as they should, the entire economy would be far stronger than it is now – and the Japanese would be trooping here to find out how it was done. So, why isn't that the case?

We are convinced that one of the primary reasons why more companies do not succeed in their business objectives lies in how they perceive and react to their market-places. We say that on the basis of both observation and personal experience (on the basis of professional/chief executive and journalist/entrepreneur respectively) and on a mass of research by academics and practitioners on both sides of the Atlantic.

This book aims to explore the marketing credo – the set of beliefs, values, attitudes and behaviours that make up a marketing approach – of a selection of companies carefully chosen to provide a cross-section of the best in British marketing. It does not confine its researches to purely British-owned companies. The sole criterion for inclusion has been proven excellence in marketing.

It was business writer Theodore (Ted) Levitt who coined the term 'marketing myopia' to explain how apparently competent managers failed to see the shifting sands around their products. In fiercely competitive international markets myopia can all too often be a fatal affliction. Some of the companies in our sample have had this condition and sought treatment successfully. They can testify that correcting faulty marketing vision is a lot more difficult than buying a pair of spectacles. Others seem to have had 20/20 marketing vision from their beginnings. Call them lucky if you like – but in business most luck is earned by intensive application of basic principles.

'The central task of business is to get and keep a customer,' says

1

Levitt. It is a theme echoed by almost every other well-known business writer. 'There is only one valid definition of business purpose – to create a customer,' says Peter Drucker. 'Markets don't buy anything – customers do,' declares Tom Peters in *A Passion for Excellence*. Yet this simple fact seems to be lost on so many businesses, whether brash and new or mature and experienced. The most frequent reason for the failure of new companies, for example, is not that they have a bad product. It is simply that they have not checked that there is a need for the product; that it provides a greater benefit than competing products; or that the potential customers are identified and informed of the product and what it can do for them.

Similarly, established companies fail because they have not identified changes in what the market wants; because they have not reacted to or forestalled the introduction of something better by their competitors; or because they were unaware that technology or social developments were making the basis of their businesses as obsolete as the buggy whip, the adding machine, the ear trumpet or the separate collar.

The great success stories are about people who identified needs for products and exploited them in a creative way, like the copying machine, the ballpoint pen, the safety razor, the credit card, the aerosol, the packaged holiday. They are also about people who, having met a market demand once, continue to innovate by maintaining close relationships with their customers.

The reason for failure is seldom lack of investment. Indeed, many successful companies during the last few years have added to their success by buying newer manufacturing plant cheaply, from competitors who had gone bankrupt because they had lost touch with changing markets.

Major groups have been built by market-alert companies acquiring businesses which had lost their way in the market-place, even though they had sound assets and brand names. The appeal to shareholders in recent takeover battles has been primarily on the claim that the predator would be much more effective in the market-place than the victim was.

Much has been written over the years about how to succeed in the market-place, about the marketing concept, the marketing mix, and how to do market research, design and develop products, package, advertise, merchandise, sell and all the others. Universities, business schools and colleges are turning out bright people with marketing qualifications, and companies are sending executives on training programmes to improve their performance. There is a wide body of marketing knowledge and research data in all the developed industrial countries. Yet in most Western economies only a limited number of companies would even claim to be good at marketing. Unfortunately this proved to be only too true when international competition became really tough in the 1970s and 1980s. To Western companies' shame, they were often bested by companies from countries such as Japan which were regarded as having little marketing tradition or sophistication in the domestic or the international market-place.

Significantly, Japan's domestic market-place is not only tough on importers. Ruthless competition in the home market has forced companies to treat marketing, in its broadest sense, with deadly seriousness. The Japanese products that burst out on the international stage, so dramatically wrapping up Western competition, have all been tried and tested at home in what is probably the toughest market-place in the world.

So the reason for poor marketing performance is not lack of available information, nor is it lack of a marketing or trading tradition. Trading is as old as man himself and the purpose is basically as it always was, despite being sophisticated and jargonized into marketing. Some people, and indeed some nations, have always been better at it than others. Even social systems and political philosophies have been built around it. Wars have been fought and empires have fallen because of it. Fortunes have been made, careers and lives have been lost on it. It is an integral part of primitive and developed societies and it is as central to the Bible as it is to *The Wealth of Nations* and *Das Kapital*. In some societies, like the UK, it has been frowned upon and disparaged, socially and educationally. Over the last forty years the USA, and more recently Japan, have been its leading exponents.

Now, in the UK and Europe particularly, excellence in marketing is acknowledged as essential to corporate and national prosperity. The improvements in manufacturing performance from investment in new technology, modern plant, higher productivity, cost control, better manning levels and enlightened industrial relations have brought a level of cost competitiveness unknown for decades. They

3

have also brought the realization that this by itself is not enough to achieve success.

Customers do not normally buy on price except when the product is either a commodity or is not sufficiently different to influence choice.

Cost competitiveness has to be translated into market-place advantage. That requires the marketing thinking and disciplines which have kept some companies consistently strong and successful in the market-place, or enabled them to survive through deep recessions, or come back from near disasters.

This book is about that kind of marketing excellence. It looks at companies in three main sectors – service, consumer goods and industrial – and in fourteen business areas. It aims to throw light upon how effective marketing – a marketing culture, if you will – helps yesterday's company to retain its vitality today and today's company to thrive into tomorrow.

The method we have chosen is to consider the significance of pairs of companies, who are in the same business but who are achieving marketing success in what may appear to be quite different ways. From these similarities and differences we have drawn a number of lessons about what makes an effective marketing culture. Or to put it another way, we have attempted to answer the question: 'What are the basics of marketing excellence?'

The companies are:

TSB	Abbey National
British Airways	British Caledonian
Saatchi & Saatchi	Ogilvy & Mather
Hertz	Avis
Bird's Eye Walls	Smith's Crisps
Cadbury	Rowntree Mackintosh
Schweppes	Beecham Drinks
Beecham Toiletries	Johnson & Johnson
C. & J. Clark	Hi-Tec Sports
Jaguar	BMW
Black & Decker	3M
Ever Ready	Duracell
IBM	ICL
JCB	Lansing

4

They are, in most cases, nationally or internationally known companies, or have some particular feature that merits their inclusion. They range from multinationals to family-controlled businesses, large and small, subsidiaries and divisions. In addition to those examined in detailed discussion with chief executives and marketing directors, we also refer to others where the authors have personal knowledge or experience. Some further supporting information has also come from a few organizations where the enquiry was more limited and in some cases primarily from company publications.

Marketing is an activity which fascinates some, frightens a few, and frustrates many. It has its champions, its charlatans and its critics; and claims about it range from management panacea to academic futility.

Marketing can benefit from sound academic probing and the resulting bank of fundamental data. At the end of the day, however, its real worth will be judged by how it helps companies to win against severe domestic and international competition, and the strategic weapons it provides to achieve this success.

We are not concerned with the individual elements of market research, product development, promotional activities, advertising spend or sales-force management, which are covered in many excellent textbooks, and which in any case depend on the circumstances of the particular market. We probe much more fundamental issues, such as:

Mission and objectives of the business.
Chief executive and board orientation, attitudes and background.
Short/long-term goals and where the emphasis is placed.
Company organization and culture.

Knowledge/understanding/segmentation of markets.
Analysis of competitors and what makes them tick.
Statement of marketing strategy, objectives and competitive edge.
Development/creativity/positioning of products and services.

People – selection, training and motivation.
Communication of strategy/objectives.
Commitment to achievement.
Measuring/rewarding marketing performance.

This book attempts to distil the driving force behind consistent marketing success, and considers how other companies can rise to similarly high performance levels through the practical application of the culture, creativity and commitment demonstrated by these masters of the market-place. By this we do not mean that all successful companies have the same culture and values – far from it, as our examples will show. Successful companies create their own values, appropriate to their own markets and circumstances, and it is the ability to do so in a purposeful, effective manner that sets them apart from those who never quite seem to achieve that essential rapport with their markets.

All the companies we have studied in this project have a clear understanding not just that marketing is important, but of why it is important. At all levels and functions of management, people *live* for their markets. They have what we can only describe as a marketing credo. Unlike most credos or strongly held beliefs, the marketing credo does not stifle innovation or initiative. These companies have made marketing the foundation stone of their business, recognizing that, in the end, everything a company does or fails to do has an impact on its market-place.

To explore these issues, we have divided this book into three sections. In the first we identify the similarities and dissimilarities of companies which have achieved success in the same market-place. In the second section, we attempt to draw out the commonalities in the marketing approach and culture across all twenty-eight companies. Finally we aim to condense these common factors into a smaller number of fundamental elements that any company can focus upon.

PART ONE

THE COMPANIES

Services

FINANCIAL SERVICES

The Trustee Savings Bank   The Abbey National Building Society

Across the world the artificial barrier between banks, insurance companies, building societies, unit trusts and stockbrokers – to name but a few – are collapsing. They are now having to redefine themselves as being in the *financial services* sector, as each finds itself able to poach on territories formerly denied to it. Financial institutions in the UK are likely to feel the effects of this upheaval far more keenly than their US counterparts.

The key to survival in such an environment lies in swift response to customer needs. Here's how consultant Derek Furby reported the situation, as discussed at a recent international symposium in Switzerland:

Banks tend to take their customers for granted. In the corporate sector, account officers frequently call on customers inadequately briefed about their operations and plans and their potential need for banking services. In some cases they are not even aware of contacts that individual customers may have with other colleagues in their bank.

Branches, in many countries, continue to present a forbidding aspect to retail customers, both in terms of location, layout, facilities available within the branch and hours of business.

As a result of this customer neglect it has been relatively easy for competition, often from non-traditional sources, to make inroads into the market-place. The impact of increased competition has forced many bankers to reassess their service standards. If they are to understand and respond to customer needs, most banks will have to do more market research, analyse the results and act on the findings.

The banks who do so will be far better placed to develop appropriate products and service standards to match and thus gain a significant competitive advantage. Successful banks will need to be able to create a perception of value and this can only be done by understanding what customers' values are. The same message occurs in Stephen Davis's global study *Excellence in Banking*. Says Davis:

> The excellent banks have been driven by their customers to re-evaluate their client priorities, organisational structure, information base and delivery systems. They are much closer to their customers in the sense of physical contact, formal and informal market research and the use of relationship managers who are assuming an increasingly important role in customer interface.

As Nikolaus Senn of Union Bank of Switzerland puts it: 'Banking is where the customer is.'

Over the last ten years the high-street banks have changed their whole approach to customers and to the range of services they offer. There is a continual flood of new services for both retail and corporate customers, covering everything from credit cards and personal loans to insurance, investment and mortgages.

Building societies have responded to the threat to their traditional mortgage business and moved into the auto tills, cards and cheque books, and have taken account of the Building Societies Act which gave them freedom within specified parameters to move outside their basic home-loan business. In this highly competitive financial services market, two organizations, The Trustee Savings Bank and The Abbey National Building Society, stand out for different reasons.

The TSBs were traditionally associated with working-class, small depositors, and seen as somewhat philanthropic, unexciting and very dependable. When the Page Committee in the early 1970s gave the TSBs freedom to offer a wide range of financial services, the whole scene changed. They began increasingly to rival and surpass what the high-street banks were offering. In the west country, for example, they seized the initiative to capture a significant slice of the emerging boom in small-business loans.

As it waited for privatization the TSB in England and Wales consolidated the transformation achieved over the last ten years. It has changed the attitudes and approach of management and staff. It has widened the services on offer, introducing new, real-time technology on account statements, building a massive personal customer base and credit-card operation and moving into commercial business.

Branch managers have had to undergo a culture change and are now actively selling the services available to commercial and personal customers.

TSB has carried out extensive market and customer research to identify the needs of existing customers, who are primarily in the C2 DE categories. This sector is potentially faster growing than the ABs, who represent the bulk of competitors' customers.

From this research, the TSB has developed custom-built services and products to meet the needs it has identified. Among those needs is living up to the critically important image of being a personal bank which genuinely cares for its customers.

Blending this concern with positive selling of TSB services takes considerable skill and justifies the emphasis on having the right people, properly trained. TSB has emerged as a strong, thrusting, market-oriented bank with clearly researched objectives and a conviction from top to bottom that it has a winning combination.

Leading TSB England and Wales is chief general manager Leslie Priestley, who came to the job with a highly impressive track record at Barclays Bank, including the launch of Barclaycard, overall responsibility for Barclays' marketing and the management of the largest life broker in the UK, Barclays Insurance Services Company.

In his view, personal customer service is paramount and TSB has to create outstanding managers dedicated to looking after personal customers. This attitude is illustrated very effectively by the simple fact that TSB counters normally have more manned tills than any other bank, with book-keeping carried out at the counters. In other banks many cashiers also work in the book-keeping department, which means they are pulled off the counters to the detriment of customer service.

TSB is building on its strengths and its traditional recognition as a bank specializing in the personal customer market, by offering a warm, friendly and efficient service to the individual. These basic qualities, coupled with latest technology, are now being applied to the commercial market as TSB seeks to broaden its business base.

In the last few years TSB has recognized the importance of developing services tailored to individual professions and industries. With its strong branch network and well-trained and committed

staff who are aware of local needs, innovation based on understanding of those needs will be the hallmark of the TSB's future
development.

Market segmentation based on customer analysis and careful positioning of products is clearly seen in its identification of the increasingly important customers in the sixty-plus age-group market. TSB is
endowed with a high proportion of elderly customers and has
services specifically geared to this segment, including savings plans,
life insurance, special annuities, investment and travel facilities.

As the competition increases in intensity, TSB's sensitivity to the
changing life style and interests of particular customer segments
(such as people preparing for retirement) and to the creation of the
right packages to meet the needs of those segments will bring a new
dimension to its personal customer service.

Over the last fifteen years building societies have attracted depositors
away from banks to the extent that over 50% of people's personal
liquid assets are invested with building society accounts.

Within the building society movement, deposits have also been
increasingly concentrated in the hands of the top ten out of nearly two
hundred societies. The top ten control over three-quarters of society
assets.

The Abbey National Building Society is the second-largest and has
been in the vanguard of this growth, with its assets increasing
elevenfold since 1970. It has almost eight million deposit accounts
and nearly one million borrowers, and its customer profile differs
significantly from TSB, with an orientation towards the twenty-one
to thirty-four-year age group and the higher ABC1 socio-economic
groups, as opposed to TSB's forty-five-plus and C2 DE groups.

The Abbey National began to demonstrate its maverick inclinations most noticeably in Clive Thornton's period as chief executive
late in the 1970s and early 1980s. This was skilfully modified to a
reputation for innovation – an interesting reflection of the market
orientation of a chief executive with a legal background. It also illustrated the basic fact that effective marketing pervades the entire
organization and that attention-grabbing publicity is no substitute for
it.

Peter Birch became chief executive in 1984 following a successful
career with Gillette in marketing and general management. He

brought strategic and business planning, with the associated financial objectives and disciplines, to an organization which had tended to operate in an entrepreneurial but unstructured mode.

The mission of the society is to achieve controlled growth with the increased profit margins necessary to strengthen reserves, in readiness for the operational freedom which will come from the 1987 Building Societies Act.

In the dramatically changed environment of the last few years, profit margins at Abbey National have come under pressure from three factors:

Highly competitive interest rates have changed the deposit structure towards high-rate accounts and away from ordinary shares, to a very marked extent.

Competition from banks has reduced societies' ability to raise interest rates and forced them to eliminate previous premiums on larger and endowment mortgages.

Management fees have increased and taken a greater share of a reduced margin which, with increased liability to corporation tax, reduced profitability very substantially in 1984.

This profit pressure underlined the need for the management and financial disciplines which have been introduced, the branch profitability statements and the elimination of unnecessary agency fees. It also increased the need for innovation in technology, to reduce costs and provide improved customer service; and creative marketing to generate the right type and volume of business.

Just as TSB has exploited its opposite strengths and market segments, Abbey National sees its younger age group, higher income, prosperous south-east customer profile as a major competitive edge, especially in the present difficult economic environment.

Abbey National sees itself as a marketing driven, financially oriented organization, and invests heavily in researching the needs and attitudes of its customers, competitors and staff. Economic, lifestyle, product and operational technology research has given it a deep understanding of the market. This has enabled it to couple its traditional appeal as the safe investment, middle of the road fair dealer with that of a progressive, go-ahead, technologically innovative organization. It has frequently led the field with developments like the mortgage certificate (which represents the next best thing to an actual mortgage) and its Abbeylink service (which provides the

facility to deposit, withdraw and check the account balance automatically, seven days a week, twenty-four hours each day, free of
charge). Abbey intends to instal its automatic teller machines in
retail stores as well as its own branches and is continuing to set a
fierce pace for its competitors. Most of these are still coming to
terms with other Abbey National innovations – for example, the
first cheque account operated by a building society; the Abbey
National Property Service, which provides a nationwide estate
agency service using seven hundred independent agencies; and the
Abbey Housing Association Ltd, which builds homes or assists
self-build groups, particularly in inner city areas.

The imaginative awareness of what is needed in the market is
extended to the calibre and competence of the Abbey staff involved
with customers. Selecting people carefully and developing them
through tailor-made training is an integral part of the business
planning, and applies from top to bottom.

Abbey National's move to performance-related rewards, based on
clearly defined objectives, reflects its commitment to beating the
competition it will meet in the bigger, wider markets it will have
in the future when the present restrictions are removed.

Abbey National intends to stick to its market, which is finance
for homes and the people who live in them. The depth of its market
research and concern for what makes its customers tick is remarkable. For example, research into the importance of instant access to
funds versus high interest rates also goes into detail on *why* people
sometimes need swift access. That particular piece of research
showed that some 40% of people in this country consider they
could become redundant – a startling reflection on the new enterprise society we are creating.

AIRLINES

British Airways   **British Caledonian**

The airline business is probably the most complex in our study in
terms of market influences. Companies in this sector have to take
into consideration factors such as care, comfort, anxiety, cost,

international regulations, safety, political influence, terrorism and weather, to name but a few.

The reasons why people fly at all and why they choose to fly with particular airlines are equally complex; and in such a market environment, being successful requires particular talents.

The problems airlines face are threefold. One is the ubiquitous issue of costs and margins. Until 1985 rising fuel costs and over-capacity forced airlines to seek cost-effectiveness measures to survive. In all too many cases the method they chose was a reduction in the quality of the service they provided. Significantly, those who are prospering now are those who recognized that you cannot compromise on service quality and retain market position. The second problem relates to the age and composition of fleets. Those companies that read their future markets properly were able to order planes of the right capacity for the right routes, giving themselves a significant competitive edge in cost terms.

The third problem is that air travel has become largely a commodity. The planes, the departure and arrival facilities, the seating and the length of flights do not vary greatly between airlines. Intergovernmental agreements mean that in many cases even the price is the same. The airlines that succeed are those that manage to differentiate their product from the mass.

All of these are, in essence, marketing issues.

British Airways is a major international airline which has undergone a basic transformation over the last three years. British Caledonian is in world terms quite a small company, but has a public image which belies its real size. It has survived and grown in one of the world's most competitive markets.

The British Airways' corporate goal is quite simply to be the best and most successful airline in the world. Chairman Lord King and chief executive Colin Marshall and their managers are determined to achieve this goal. Their corporate objectives are just as bold, and include:

Providing the highest levels of service to all customers, direct and indirect.

Preserving high professional and technical standards to achieve the highest levels of safety.

Providing a uniform image worldwide and maintaining a specific set of standards for each clearly defined market segment.

Responding quickly and sensitively to the changing needs of present and potential customers.

Managing, operating and marketing the airline in the most efficient manner.

Creating a service and people-oriented work environment.

Earning a profit sufficient to provide an acceptable return on assets.

This wasn't always the case. Just a few years ago, before the airline crisis of the late 1970s and early 1980s, British Airways fared badly in independent surveys of air travellers. The only difference between Air France and BA, ran the joke, was that the French air hostesses made it absolutely plain that the customers were a nuisance, while the BA hostesses simply ignored them. Insofar as BA is concerned, those quips seem pretty silly now.

Over little more than three years Colin Marshall has changed BA from an operations-driven to a customer-driven organization, and the change has impacted on all aspects of the business. During this time it has also produced record operating results, survived potentially destructive litigation and prepared itself for privatization.

The impetus was survival. Deregulation in the United States looked – and still looks – like happening in Europe. Under these circumstances competition would increase even more. BA's strategy had been to follow the pack, trying to meet the demands of all market segments, responding to price challenges whenever necessary and often paying for them by reducing services. But the greater the price competition, the higher the load factor (percentage of available seats filled) needed for a route to remain viable. At the same time the annual growth in passenger traffic had slumped from 13% to 7%. (It is predicted to fall to 5% during the 1990s.)

Suddenly the airline market was a whole new game. As Marshall expressed it at a recent presentation:

As a result of all these influences the market today has taken on a new character, breaking free from the controls of earlier years.

—More airlines competing on the same routes.

—New airlines creating new market opportunities.

—Customer demands for higher services standards.

Unfortunately at the same time expectations are lower. From 1973–83 market growth has slowed to 7% per annum, and growth through to the 90s is expected to be around 5%.

Customers are more discerning, partly from experience and partly from the increased choice available. They want more and better service and they frequently want lower fares.

The result of these influences is that the market place is now much more volatile – customers' demands and preferences change more rapidly – increasing the challenge to airlines that wish to serve the market successfully. Airlines must study the customer carefully to understand his wants, and then act swiftly to provide what is needed. Innovation may not always pay off.

The market place forces now operating often pull in different directions making the job of the airline more difficult than ever before. Success will be achieved only by those airlines which identify changing demands correctly, whilst balancing this with the need to produce better profit levels.

To be fair to the previous management, it had already begun to make many of the changes that were needed to change the orientation of the airline towards the market-place and away from operations. But radical change within a large organization usually demands a new broom. Marshall's first step was to create well-defined objectives in each area of the business and an organization restructured with clear responsibilities to achieve them. Extensive research segmented the markets and identified needs, attitudes, life styles and critical elements in each one. For business travellers, what scored highest were schedule times (and meeting them), comfort and in-flight attention. A substantial percentage of these passengers came in the 'white knuckles at take-off' category. In the same way, the leisure and charter markets were researched to determine what was really important for these relatively infrequent travellers.

Competitors were checked out in detail against the research results and rated against checks on BA's own performance.

Out of this in-depth analysis of markets, customers, competitors and BA's own staff came the development of the new culture, which was oriented straight at service to customers. This provided the core of the competitive edge which was going to transform BA into the best airline in the world.

Extensive training programmes were carried through under the slogan Putting People First. The programmes combined the objectives of enabling different groups of employees to appreciate their interdependence upon one another, and of focusing the airline's attention on the customer's needs. Over twenty thousand employees with direct customer contact have attended these courses, which have now been extended to cover key personnel in travel agencies. Similar programmes for staff who do not have direct customer contact promote the need to provide the necessary support for those staff who are in regular contact with the public.

The corporate livery and logo were redesigned to project the changed philosophy and the new, confident public face BA was presenting. The company introduced new products, including super shuttle in the UK, super club internationally and the development of the Oasis lounge facility offering London transit services.

Top management placed strong emphasis on communicating to staff the reasons for what was being done, and that success would not only safeguard the future of BA but would provide direct financial benefits to them. The response has been positive and was highlighted by Colin Marshall as one of the reasons for the very considerable turn-around which has been achieved.

In his view the reasons were:

Clear objectives and commitment to achieving them.
Dedication, loyalty and response of staff.
Sense of purpose and pride in the airline.
Open communication throughout the organization.
Sound management controls on all business operations.
Customer First – A Way of Life.

Research is confirming that customers are perceiving the service improvements, both on the ground and in the air, which have been tailor-made to suit their requirements. Staff also enjoy their participation in the improvement process.

The airline has won a wide range of awards for excellence in various fields of activity, including the Queen's Award for Export, advertising awards, business traveller awards, cabin staff awards and travel agent awards.

BA's financial results confirm that the new corporate way of life is working, and has made possible further heavy investment in new aircraft and equipment to support what is being achieved in its markets around the world.

Becoming the best airline in the world means putting the customer first in everything the company does. The fact that in 1985 BA flew more people to more countries, more profitably than any other airline, would suggest that Colin Marshall has got it right.

'British Caledonian is the airline which strives to provide business travellers with the best in personal service. We have long recognized that the world business community demands a distinct brand of airline service tailored to its very specific requirements,' says David Coltman, managing director of B.Cal.

This clear statement of the airline's mission stems from the philosophy of the present chairman, Sir Adam Thompson, who founded Caledonian Airways in 1961. From the beginning, serving the customer has been the number-one priority, the central tenet of the organization and operations of B.Cal.

The last eight years have been a period of furious growth for the company. It aims to consolidate this expansion, achieve a secure place in the airline business and weave its way through the minefield of political and legislative influences which will continue to affect the air travel business.

To survive against major airlines that have more hardware, more routes or more political backing, B.Cal. analysed the markets in depth. It determined that the business traveller was its prime customer segment. Since it had nothing distinctive to offer in aircraft hardware, it decided to concentrate on software. That required detailed knowledge of what the customer considered important, and what the competition was offering.

Major investment went into researching the business traveller segment. This showed that quality rather than cost was the critical element. Psychological research indicated that fear, uncertainty or stress in flying could affect nearly three-quarters of passengers, and this emphasized the need to help customers relax and feel they were being looked after. It underlined the importance of an airline taking responsibility for the maximum period of the travelling time, ideally looking after its passengers from door to door.

The product which airlines sell is intangible. To obtain a grasp on it, B.Cal. had to identify the most important factors in flying, collect personal information on passengers and establish a personal relationship with them. Attitudes to B.Cal. were probed and compared with the ideal and with attitudes towards competitors. The image

19

that emerged was a caring, warm, friendly airline giving personal service. (There was also a clear indication of admiration for the independent underdog.) It was also apparent that B.Cal. was seen as a larger organization than it really was.

B.Cal. concentrated its product development on business passengers, with emphasis on reassurance and being looked after, personified in the Caledonian Girls; on quality of care and service rather than price; and on understanding, closeness and personal attention.

B.Cal. is well aware of the pressures the business traveller is under to complete his business in the minimum time and with the least inconvenience. Two distinct brands of service, first-class and super-executive, were created to match these requirements and designed to ensure that travellers reached their destination in the best possible condition, both physically and mentally.

The tartan-clad staff of B.Cal. is perhaps its most visible asset, and they epitomize the airline's friendly yet professional attitude. Training in this environment is of critical importance. B.Cal. puts considerable effort both into the key factors in passenger care and service, and into the development of executives and staff to meet future needs.

B.Cal. has a simple, single-minded commitment to being the first-choice airline for business travellers. For years this has been encapsulated in the firm corporate statement: 'We never forget you have a choice.' It is intended, and is claimed to be, the spur to B.Cal. staff to provide, both on the ground and in the air, a level of courteous personal service unmatched in the world.

Creating a product differential to provide a competitive edge is extremely difficult in the international airline business but B.Cal. appears to have achieved it with its tartan-clad 'software'. Its technical hardware appears to be pretty competitive too, and top management's sights are set on further expansion.

ADVERTISING AGENCIES

Saatchi & Saatchi   **Ogilvy & Mather**

The cobbler's children syndrome is particularly appropriate to the advertising business. Agencies frequently exhort their clients to define clearly what their markets are, their objectives within the markets, and how they intend to achieve them. These same clients might be very surprised at the answers if they were to ask some of the agencies the same questions. Their reactions might well draw the observation that creativity and business management can be uncomfortable bedfellows.

The highly successful major agencies have learned this lesson, and two in particular, Saatchi & Saatchi and Ogilvy & Mather, are good examples of companies which operate their businesses on the same tightly managed, market oriented basis as do their best clients.

Saatchi & Saatchi was dedicated to growth from its formation in 1970, when its clearly defined objective was to be the world's biggest and most profitable agency, via the strategy of being the most creative. This company is not lacking in ambition. Recently, via a string of acquisitions on both sides of the Atlantic, it has pursued a policy of becoming a global business services company, offering a total range of services from management consultancy to design. Its growth by acquisition has been so fast and furious that *Business* magazine recently ran a front-page story referring to the company as Snaatchit & Snaatchit. A survey in January 1985 posted Saatchi as having the highest earnings per share of all the top one hundred British companies over the previous five years.

Saatchi & Saatchi identified the special needs of multinational business operations and global marketing, and set out its stall to match those needs.

It has a financial orientation and strong commercial attitudes. These pervade an organization structured to achieve business now, and to meet the needs of the future growth to which it is committed. In 1981 it became the largest agency in Europe and it is now the seventh-largest in the world.

Terry Bannister, the joint managing director, considers that good luck is important in this business. Luck certainly ran for Saatchi. It learned from the early acquisition mistakes that the S&S whiz kids were not to everyone's liking. After an early major takeover it contacted the clients to tell them what would be happening and nearly lost many accounts. From that experience it learned two lessons – humility, and the supremacy of the client.

Saatchi believes that its prospects turn largely on its ability to apply to itself the same disciplines that it recommends to its clients

21

for their brands. That is, to be sharp in the definition of long-term objectives, frank about strengths and weaknesses, clear about position in the market and sure about the quality of the product. It believes it will make progress in the market-place only if it offers something better than the competition. It also saw early on in its spectacular growth that there was considerable value in establishing a clear brand image for its own services.

Every annual report from the first year has stressed this requirement. Saatchi sets the standard – unachievable perhaps, but none the less the kind of goal to motivate and challenge creative staff – that every thirty seconds of commercial it makes for a client should be worth sixty seconds from a competitor. It tells the world that it has a belief in excellence – that in all spheres of life and at all times there will be a few performances which are excellent, a few which are very poor ... while the majority will be just average.

> Our aim in all of our activities and at all times is the avoidance of the average and achievement of the excellent. This applies to all aspects of the way we run our business – to the people we employ, to the advertising we run, to the way we buy our media, to the operating margins we expect.
>
> All our standards are set by the 'norm' – whatever that is, by definition, there is a better way.

Market information and competitive intelligence have a high priority in Saatchi's own business and for its clients, since they allow opportunism and fast decisive moves – essential elements in their dynamic market environment.

This basic, realistic approach extends to the products produced for clients. An advertising campaign succeeds only if it ultimately helps to create new sales for the client, and does so effectively and economically. Moreover, advertising cannot create sales unless it catches the consumer's attention, changes his attitudes and stimulates a purchase. Image and brand awareness are meaningless if they fail to achieve greater turnover. Saatchi considers a creative ad an exercise in self-indulgence unless it achieves the client's marketing objectives.

Saatchi has also identified the growing demand for other marketing and consultancy services, as client companies have slimmed down dramatically over the last few years of business recession and have reverted to buying in specialist support services.

The management of its business is essentially simple, with autonomous business units responsible to a parent company, which sets basic financial policies and goals but lets the operating company management get on with running the business and staying close to its customers.

In the advertising business, there are two basic types of agency: the small highly creative ones who resist management disciplines, which they consider will blunt creativity; and the very large ones which are often creatively dull, since the systems and structures they have introduced tend towards bureaucracy, which stifles creativity.

Saatchi has managed to combine the advantages and business disciplines of a multinational organization with creativity in depth. This is its competitive advantage, and a growing list of international blue-chip clients is evidence of its success.

With total commitment from the chairman downwards, the demand for high performance from staff and the appeal such a working environment has for 'winners', Saatchi & Saatchi may have created the unique agency which has eluded the others who have tried – a size which provides a stability and extensive back-up to clients but also retains the innovative creativity essential for success.

This would be in keeping with its flair for taking developments over the previously accepted horizons, breaking new ground and going just that little bit further than the others – if only because someone has to.

Ogilvy & Mather was founded by David Ogilvy in 1948, well in advance of Saatchi's, and to a considerable extent set the example Saatchi has followed. O&M Worldwide is now the fourth largest advertising agency in the world, but the principles on which it operates are basically the same as those David Ogilvy established. These were: research, professional discipline, creative brilliance and getting results.

Its objective now is to be the best advertising agency, not the biggest; on the basis that size in itself is no benefit once an agency is big enough to handle big accounts.

The main purposes are defined as:

To serve its clients more effectively than any other agency.

To run the agency with a sense of competitive urgency, majoring on its strengths and striving for excellence.

To maintain the commitment to outstanding, creative work.

To earn a significant increase in profit each year.

To make O&M the most exciting agency in which to work.

Within O&M there is widespread acceptance of this ethos and the company is managed as a brand, following the same principles and disciplines that would be applied to a client's brand. The organization has a flexible structure to cater for the specific needs of existing clients and new business development is run as a separate operation to give it the individual attention and management style it needs.

Business objectives are spelt out clearly and the management controls operate as they would in O&M's best client companies. This tight strategy does not inhibit creativity – indeed, the worldwide creative head, Norman Berry, is often quoted as saying, 'Give me the freedom of a tightly defined strategy.' The most effective creativity seems to come from giving people a framework in which to innovate.

O&M is concerned with providing better, more effective advertising. The basis of this is its client strategy blueprint. It starts with how consumers make decisions. The research sharpens strategies and provides creative people with the freedom to do their work. The strategy blueprint is the O&M approach to defining and refining client strategies, based on O&M's extensive research into understanding how consumers make decisions and how advertising works. O&M considers it an essential prerequisite on which to base the whole advertising process and it is used throughout the O&M world.

The strategy blueprint system underpins another basic approach to client service – providing clients with a single source for all the creative communications skills needed to make their market respond, rather than just advertising. This is the Ogilvy orchestration: a commitment to deliver a full arsenal of excellent services, separately and in combination. Not surprisingly, the research done by both Saatchi and O&M has prompted similar solutions, although, again not surprisingly, they are presented in quite different ways.

Despite O&M's history and the emphasis placed by its founder on the importance of learning and teaching, it is still surprising just how

strongly training and communications programmes figure throughout the organization, and how strongly senior management is committed to giving its time to these programmes. The careful selection of
young people to join the company is another part of creating the O&M
culture. Top management believes that excellence and stability in a
high-risk business are jeopardized if the company fails to hire the
right people.

The attitude to rewarding performance is similarly creative and
based on meeting personal preferences within a specified cost. O&M
executives have a tangible worth to the company. The way this is
reflected in remuneration terms is both flexible and tailored to individual values. For example, it matters not if part of that remuneration
takes the form of a Porsche in one case and a chauffeur-driven car in
another. O&M seeks to retain people who are motivated by the
demands of excellence, who understand balanced judgement and
decision making, have mental agility rather than depth of intellect,
emotional self-confidence and the ability to communicate.

The company tries to create an environment in which creative
judgement flourishes and can be managed. At the end of the day, a
passionate commitment to succeed competitively is also essential,
and it is not surprising that only a limited number of these paragons
emerge from the O&M production line. However, the ones who do
have produced outstanding performances. The size of the UK company doubled and profits trebled in the four years prior to 1986, an
exceptional achievement by any standards.

O&M's priority is to grow with existing clients and much of its
success has come from this commitment. However, the basic business principles on which it manages require a planned amount of
new business. Establishing new business development as a separate
operation is a measure of the importance the company attaches to this
source of growth.

Some £4.5 billion is spent on advertising in the UK each year. No
single agency has more than 4% of the total, so there is plenty of scope
for market-share improvement. In fact, with such a fragmented
market the scope for dramatic growth by the high-flying agencies
would be the envy of companies in most other UK business sectors.

There are also significant changes coming, with new media
developments enabling consumers to be more selective about what
they watch and read. Audiences will become more fragmented, as

will their life styles, and the increasingly diverse demands on agencies and their capabilities are likely to confirm the wisdom of what Saatchi's and O&M are trying to achieve.

Says Michael Baulk, O&M's managing director, 'The future looks very good indeed; good for advertising and good for O&M – if we remember the fundamentals of our business and we practise them with skill and consistency.'

CAR HIRE

Hertz   **Avis**

The car-rental business is complex and extremely competitive with over two thousand companies offering a wide range of vehicles and prices. Most customers are car owners, so unlike when they deal with other service industries (e.g. hotels or flying) they have something to compare with the rented product.

The market has a major business content with large customers exercising considerable bargaining muscle in what can easily become a commodity market. It is also international, with all the logistical, cultural and financial influences that implies.

Hertz is the largest car-rental business in the world, and has been established in the UK some forty years in self-drive rental, and about eight years in leasing. In the late 1970s and early 1980s margins on self-drive rental, which were already poor, were further depressed because the industry's prime competitive stance was on rental rates.

Data on the market size and growth rate was not comprehensive and tended to be available primarily from airports or credit-card companies. In the early 1980s, with the recession aggravating profitability pressures, a new general management with marketing and sales background changed Hertz from primarily a financially managed company to one led by a market-driven strategy.

The company mission was to achieve an acceptable return on assets employed in the business. It aimed to do this by developing market and customer understanding, and by turning the whole organization into a selling vehicle. This strategy required market segmentation and a rifle-shot approach to performance-influenced segments. Research was carried out to identify the image of and attitudes towards Hertz and its main competitor, Avis. The results indicated the strengths and weaknesses of Hertz, what features were considered important, and how attitudes differed, depending on whether the hire was for business (where reliability was important) or for leisure (where the emphasis was on safety). Among the factors rated were the influence of staff attitudes, speed of processing and ease of documentation. These provided the raw material which was translated into new products, tailored to clearly identified market segments.

Hertz launched its Business Class, aimed directly at the performance-influenced businessman, and offering vehicles from the middle of the range upwards, lowest mileage models, extra features, a free copy of *Business Week* and preferential counter and check-in service. There was a total package charge, which made it easy for secretaries and executives to book, and a gift to make the journey that little bit more pleasant.

Similarly tailored products were developed for other selected segments such as the American vacation visitor, with attractively presented route guides, privileges with hotels and so on. Hertz concedes that some of its ideas are not original, but claims that if a competitor developed something new and appropriate, it would improve on both the product and the packaging of it.

Market segmentation, product positioning and a clearly identified competitive advantage were backed by efficient operations. The results exceeded expectations in volume and profitability.

Planning in the car-rental business is as important as it is perilous, as the wave of cancelled trips for both business and leisure markets in the wake of European terrorist outrages illustrated in 1986. Exchange rate fluctuations aggravate an already difficult situation but Hertz still expects its managers to achieve their plan objectives without fail. To ensure they do so, Hertz places heavy emphasis on branch managers' involvement in market forecasting within the established strategy; remuneration is performed linked, with each branch treated as a profit centre in its own right.

Hertz considers training to be critically important to the success of its market-driven strategy. It places the training emphasis on segments where performance, rather than purely price–volume considerations, is paramount. Branches see their role to be selling as well as carrying out operations and this attitude has been encouraged through award programmes. Staff have become much more aware of how their behaviour influences customers, and what they need to do to beat competitors. Some devolution of jurisdiction over tactical tariff adjustments has boosted their confidence and ability to take local initiatives.

The change to a market/customer orientation and the comprehensive support programme behind it have received a very positive response from both management and staff. Hertz's image research and complaints/compliments analysis indicate that they appear to have had a similar impact on customers.

The Hertz ideal employee profile in such an organization is someone who:

Has pride in doing a job well.
Has a strong recovery rate from all the pressures.
Is a self-starter, aware of opportunities.
Believes attention to detail is important.
Understands a customer's most recent experience is critical and that it is not just counter staff who have contact with customers.

UK managing director John Howard ascribes the company's recent strong improvement in its fortunes to a team now very aware of what customers want and committed to the performance necessary to provide it.

Avis has a clear and critical objective, which goes right through the whole organization. That is to be the best rental leasing company in the UK, achieved through a creative and innovative approach to satisfying customer requirements while achieving profit objectives.

The Avis attitude has a clinical element to it, particularly in its approach to market and competitor intelligence. The view of Geoff Corbett, the Avis UK managing director, is quite simply that the more the company knows about its competitors, the more easily Avis can anticipate and combat their activities, and the faster it can exploit market opportunities.

Quantitative market information comes primarily from the Airports Authority and from American Express data on car rental. Although not comprehensive, this does provide a basis for making market comparisons. It also places greater importance on awareness and attitude research about Avis and its competitors, and the identification of critically important factors such as ease of arrangements and the speed with which customers receive their cars.

The Avis product is developed out of this research and is aimed at meeting general market needs rather than specific segments, and in particular at making the car-rental operation as easy as possible for customers. The theme of trying harder pervades the company thinking and appears to be used in all areas of Avis's business.

Despite protestations to the contrary, there is little brand loyalty in the car-rental business, since the physical products from one company are fairly similar to those from another. The competitive advantage has to come from the other elements of the package and Avis is looking to technology for its edge in the market-place. One innovation is computerization to provide rapid rental and rapid return, with the customer running his charge card through the machine to confirm his reservation for a specific vehicle at the pick-up point. The agreement will be in the rental vehicle when he arrives. The return procedure is equally straightforward.

Avis's UK investment in automation follows its success in the US, where the company claims to have a competitive wedge rather than edge and maintains it is far ahead of the field. With competitors majoring on price, Avis considered it had to go the technology route, which was harder to follow. However, whereas the individual business traveller would choose the benefits technology provided, the corporate purchasing department still tries to use muscle on price. To justify its higher rates Avis tries to demonstrate that saving time is saving money.

The Avis data base also provides the opportunity for direct-mail promotion to customers, which is a less expensive form of advertising.

The translation of technology into personal customer service is Avis's ultimate goal. It sees this as its route to increased market share, which it claims to have achieved already in major corporate accounts.

Superficially Avis appears to be trying to be all things to all people in motor vehicle renting, but in reality it is segmenting markets while using the maximum number of features common to all segments. The most distinctive feature of the Avis approach is not 'trying harder', but its aggressive attitude towards competitors and towards achieving results. Its selling is based on hitting hard and early, and supporting the brand strongly.

Staff are highly motivated and identify strongly with Avis. Training is aimed at making them better at their job and more professional than their competitors. Avis's remuneration is the highest in the industry and the company makes extensive use of incentives and personal rewards. This requires top management to give a high priority to providing a clear definition and communication of objectives. The staff must also appreciate fully the importance of achieving objectives – to the company and to themselves.

The profitability of the company has improved dramatically over the last three years, due, at least in part, to the concentration on meeting customer needs. Avis intends to continue its aggressive stance at the expense of both major and minor competitors.

Consumer goods

FOODS

Bird's Eye Walls   **Smith's Crisps**

Two of the most interesting businesses in the wide-ranging food
sector are frozen foods and snacks. Both have considerable growth
potential, are central to changing life styles, and are highly
competitive. The two companies we examined were the founders of
the business in the UK. Both achieved a dominant position through
effective control of the market, and were then attacked by innovative
and aggressive competitors.

Their responses differed – as did their fortunes.

Bird's Eye, as part of Unilever, would be expected to have a
market orientation, but it was not the usual one. In the early stages of
frozen-food development, Bird's Eye dominated the market because
of the Unilever cold-storage distribution system. It controlled the
distribution, so marketing in the complete sense was hardly used,
since the company had little real competition.

As so often happens in similarly placed companies, managers
fell into the trap of believing that their market control would
go on and on. They paid little attention to the changes which were
taking place. In the 1970s, when the restrictions of retail price main-
tenance were lifted, there came an explosive growth of multiple
retailers and freezer centres, and the Bird's Eye dominance disappeared. By the late 1970s the company was under severe pressure
on market share and profitability, and the comfortable life was over.
Cost cutting, manufacturing performance improvements and
productivity increases became necessary across the company as it
faced major competitors, who had lower cost and more effective
operations.

How Bird's Eye could fail to anticipate the loss of its massive
competitive advantage in distribution is difficult to understand, but
events forced new chairman Don Angel and his colleagues to rethink

31

their whole approach to the business as it merged with the Walls ice cream company in 1981.

Clarifying objectives forced the recognition that the company was not in the frozen-food market but in frozen-food distribution and in a multitude of different frozen-food markets. Although the company had considered itself market driven, the disciplines and orientation of the chief executive and the board had not reflected this, and the cultural reorientation since 1981 appears to have been more fundamental than might have been expected.

In a business so influenced by changing life style, consumer attitudes, aggressive competition, new products and retailer power, market knowledge in depth was paramount. Substantial research investment led to a marketing strategy and focus on pillar or core brands in five key market sectors – a change from shotgun to rifle.

New products were developed for the first pillar brand – MenuMaster – launched in 1983. Other pillar brands followed, culminating in the Sweet Trolley range in 1985. The more traditional Bird's Eye strategic focus on innovation, heavy-weight advertising and commitment to product quality was integrated into the new approach.

Other elements of the new strategy were a much greater involvement with retailers in the profit performance of products in their stores and in how products were handled; substantial investment in new production facilities, aimed at becoming the lowest-cost producer; and Unilever research backing on new-concept development.

The extent of the change to the company culture is exemplified by the reaction to the 1985 COMA (Committee on Medical Aspects of Food) report, which recommended significant change in the national diet, including a reduction of fat intake and a higher proportion of fish, white meat, vegetable and fibre. Since the report, Bird's Eye has given priority to a development programme aimed at lowering the levels of fat, salt and sugar; removing all artificial colours; challenging the need for additives and maximizing naturalness in its products. It has also produced a publication for consumers giving the facts on healthy eating and the reasons for additives.

The company's determination to re-establish its overall leadership in highly competitive markets is also reflected in increased communication and training programmes aimed at ensuring that the whole organization knows what the objectives are and creating an environment in which high-level performance and going for objectives is part of the culture. The next step, to a performance-related reward system, is both natural and likely.

This anticipation of market change and eagerness to adapt to it is a far cry from the near-exclusive concern with a cold-storage distribution system, which typified the company in the 1960s and 1970s.

The Smith's Crisps experience is also one of lost opportunity and return from the brink. Founded in 1922 by Frank Smith, the business was aimed at grocers and public houses. Its short-shelf-life product called for local production units spread around the country.

The launch of Golden Wonder crisps in new, longer-life plastic packs, ready salted, distributed through supermarkets and heavily promoted, did two things. It exemplified a carefully researched and well-planned attack on a fast-growing and changing market on the one hand, and on the other a lack of awareness and concern by the company dominating the market. Smith's was slow to respond. Its reducing share of an increasing market still produced growth in volume. But it grew increasingly out of step with the changing market.

In the 1960s General Mills took a stake in the company and by the end of the decade had full control. The Smith's Food Group was born, and attempts were made at diversification into other food sectors. These were not successful and as General Mills had reservations about the snack market, it did not structure the company to exploit it.

In 1980 Huntley & Palmer took on Smith's as a wholly owned subsidiary and for the first time someone came to grips with the problems of a company which had lost its way. It had widespread, multiple production facilities for food extrusion, limited understanding of the market opportunities and no cohesive innovation strategy or real brand support to do anything about exploiting its manufacturing strengths.

In 1981 Nabisco acquired Huntley & Palmer. Smith's was still losing money. H&P accepted the challenge to return the company to profitability. It saw the potential in a company that, with its little blue salt packet, was part of the UK social fabric. The problem was not just in the market-place. There were severe cost problems, too.

Very quickly H&P cut distribution depots by more than half, reduced manufacturing units by a similar amount and people by about a third. Efficiency rose rapidly.

Nabisco was already in the crisp business through its Walker's subsidiary, so the takeover of Smith's had to be cleared by the Monopolies Commission, as together they represented about a third of the crisp market. Although the deal was approved, the two brands were operated separately. Smith's prepared to get back into the snacks business and particularly into crisps, where its share had fallen to about 14% from its dominant position in the 1960s and 1970s. Crisps at the time accounted for 60% of the total snack market.

The new mission of the company was:

To offer consistently high-quality products.
To support existing strong brands.
To introduce distinctive value-added new brands.
To utilize manufacturing expertise and strengths on extruded food items.

The company structure was made clear and simple, with a chief executive, board and organization oriented to the market and strongly competitive.

A heavy investment went into making good the shortcomings in knowledge and understanding of the markets, life style, attitude and product preference of customers; and into quality research. There was also a thorough analysis of competitors' manufacturing equipment, products, attitudes, strengths and weaknesses and strategic direction.

In such a situation and with the resources of Nabisco behind them, it was tempting for Smith's managers to research the market to death in the robotic style of many fast-moving consumer goods (FMCG) companies in the 1960s and 1970s. This was not allowed to happen and Smith's put its emphasis on disciplined research aimed at product innovation, and at concepts with a competitive advantage.

The market for own-brand crisps was growing rapidly, under-mining Smith's brand. At the same time Walker's had spread very successfully from a regional base and was cutting into traditional Smith's markets. The Smith's strategy was to increase its share of the non-crisp snack market through emphasis on strong brand positioning and new product innovation, and to hit back in the crisps sector. Quavers, introduced in 1968, was turned into its fastest growing brand and was quickly supported by other new products. As marketing director Stephen Barnett maintains, this gives the lie to the theory that food products follow short-term life cycles. In crisps, the famous blue salt packet was brought back, with its strong nostalgic appeal. In tune with the increasing health interest, it provided a choice on salt. Within a market now dominated by own-brand growth, the blue salt packet gave a unique brand distinction and appeal, and no competitor tried a 'me too'.

Smith's market share increased in both crisps and snacks, restoring the company to the number-one position in the total market, which was growing at around 4% until 1986. At this point it started to slow down, possibly because of the increasing interest in healthier eating.

Like Bird's Eye, Smith's has anticipated these changing attitudes and is placing its brand emphasis on the natural goodness of its products – low oil, zero cholesterol, high fibre, vitamins and protein, freedom from preservatives and artificial colouring, low salt or no salt.

It will be interesting to see if it can maintain the youngsters' interest in savouries, which was such a striking phenomenon in the 1950s and 1960s, as children switched from the traditional sweet preference to crisps and savoury snacks.

The change in company culture has extended to the profile of the Smith's manager. He once had no identifiable profile at all. Now he is seen as someone who gets things done within predetermined strategy, does rather than conceptualizes, is highly accountable and committed to achieving objectives, and who responds to performance-related rewards.

The company considers its training is still not as good as it should be and a planned approach is being developed to improve it.

Smith's has achieved a dramatic turnaround and is aiming to achieve the predictable and sustained growth which is the goal of the American owners.

It puts its success down to four particular factors:

Creative marketing.

Everyone going in the same direction.

Concentrating on areas where the company had expertise.
Commitment of the total management team.

With the growth in its markets slowing, and with increasing pressure
from the health diet lobby and greater competition, Smith's new
virility will be tested to the full. However, it shows all the signs of
being able to handle the challenge.

CHOCOLATE CONFECTIONERY

Cadbury   **Rowntree Mackintosh**

The confectionery business in the UK is something of a marketing
paradox. It is large – £2.5 billion annually – highly competitive, with
long-established companies and long-established brands taking the
lion's share of the market. Foreign competitors are infiltrating but
have not so far made a significant impact. New product successes are
few and there are external pressures from health lobbies.

The Cadbury name in chocolate goes back to 1831, when John
Cadbury opened a small factory to produce cocoas and drinking
chocolates. In 1879 the rapidly expanding business moved to Bourn-
ville and in 1899 Cadbury Brothers was incorporated as a limited
company.

Dairy Milk Chocolate was introduced in 1905 and the company
steadily extended its operations. It merged with J.S.Fry in 1919 to
form the British Cocoa and Chocolate Company and became increasingly international, opening factories in a number of commonwealth
countries. In 1969 Cadbury and Schweppes merged and over the next
decade acquired major confectionery and drinks companies in
Europe and America and also diversified into health and hygiene
products.

In 1985 Cadbury increased its share of the decreasing UK chocolate
market from 26% to 28% largely due to the success of Wispa, but this
success was overshadowed by heavy losses on US operations. These
are critical to one of Cadbury's major objectives, which is to increase
its current 5% share of the world chocolate market and improve its
league position to second, now held by Nestlé, which has never

cracked the UK chocolate market. Mars is far ahead in first place internationally.

The US loss was announced to a surprised City in September 1985, and the massive drop in Cadbury Schweppes Group profits it was likely to cause immediately set off a series of takeover rumours. Fortunately the company had already taken a number of major steps aimed at concentrating and strengthening its base, including the divestment of the health and hygiene division, the proposed buy-out of the tea and foods division, extensive changes in the US management and marketing strategy and a much more aggressive style in the overall management of the group and particularly in its market operations.

Chief executive Dominic Cadbury came into the role some two years ago with a marketing and sales background and complete conviction about the need for the organization to be increasingly market driven. He also had the strong view that the company would benefit from concentration on its two strong world brands, Cadbury and Schweppes, and that these should never be allowed to become boring.

The character and objectives of the group were spelt out and communication programmes arranged to make them understood and accepted throughout the organization. Central to this company statement was the emphasis on the market-place and its competitiveness, and that Cadbury Schweppes was in business to meet the needs of customers internationally. To succeed, the company had to become more competitive, operate to clear objectives, take advantage of change and be managed by people committed to these goals. The success would be measured in marketing and financial terms.

The existence of such a statement will concentrate attention on critical activities and it will no doubt be refined further to sharpen the concentration even more. In such a market-oriented environment extensive research was always carried out. But as other companies have found, the almost mechanical use of research is no longer meeting competitive needs. It takes additional flair or interpretive sensitivity to make that data strategically useful.

Competitor action and reaction has tended to be underestimated in the company (as has happened in a surprising number of other companies) and may have something to do with the long life of confectionery products and the limited number of new developments. Cadbury admits it let Rowntree in with Yorkie, but considers it returned the compliment with Wispa.

There is also increased awareness of the much greater competition from flowers, wine and similar products in the growing gift market segment, and the implications that this has for presentation and packaging.

The market strategy at Cadbury is to keep existing products fresh and interesting, to adapt their appeal to changing life styles, and to keep packaging and presentation in tune with fashion moves. Product development is assuming greater importance, but frequent introductions of new products are unlikely.

With the outstanding success of Wispa, this is not a surprising view. Its launch in 1984 halted the falling Cadbury UK market share. Within a few months it was the third most popular chocolate bar, after Mars and KitKat, both of which had been established for a mere fifty years. In 1985 Wispa had sales of over £80 million. The desire to carry this success to the US market was understandable, but once again the lesson was learned that different markets need different treatment. Supplies were shipped over from the UK but the distribution system for the test market ensured that consumers tasted products more than six months old. They were not impressed.

Cadbury appreciates the seriousness of this and its other US setbacks and accepts that it did not get its US market strategy right. It underestimated the difficulties and tried to do too many things in too short a time. Major moves have taken place, including the appointment early in 1985 of a new US chief executive who changed the management team, slimmed down the whole operation and brought in a marketing strategy more suited to the local distribution and market conditions.

Dominic Cadbury believes that with the changes in organization, emphasis on its world brands and commitment to clear objectives, Cadbury will move into a new phase of growth.

Rowntree Mackintosh has a similar history to Cadbury. Henry Rowntree acquired the cocoa and chocolate side of the William Tuke & Sons business in York in 1862. Seven years later, Rowntree & Co. was set up and over the period to 1969 when it merged with Mackintosh, the company's product range extended into fruit pastilles, gums and a variety of chocolate confectionery.

Acquisitions took Rowntree into transport and foods and into a number of European countries. As Rowntree Mackintosh, it linked with Hershey Food Corporation in the US for distribution, acquired American, French and Australian companies and established an agreement for manufacture in Japan.

Over a period of four years to 1984 non-UK business increased from 45% to 59% of the total turnover. As a result a restructuring of the management was introduced in 1985 to give operating company chief executives full responsibility for handling their markets, their competition and their people. This market orientation is also reflected in the board and the marketing background of the chairman.

In the traditional Rowntree business, the concentration was strongly on brands, to the extent that they were separately defined businesses. This is in direct contrast to the more integrated marketing strategy of Cadbury. Mars lies somewhere between the two. That fact that all three companies are highly successful in the home market suggests that the key to effective marketing does not lie in organizational structure.

Rowntree considers it is in the business of providing pleasure, happiness, romance and similar emotional satisfactions. Research therefore plays a vital role and it probes products, people's attitudes, taste, presentation and advertising in detail. With this philosophy, advertising is part of the product atmosphere and apparently peripheral elements become critical.

Competitors' products are analysed in detail for any challenge to the Rowntree approach. It considers that Cadbury left the gap for Yorkie to fill but that the Rowntree chunky bite appeal was quite different. It also questions the claim that Wispa is a direct competitor to Aero. It might even be considered more competitive with Yorkie.

Rowntree's attitude to new products is also different. It has a separate marketing director and department to handle this area – an indication of the importance it attaches to product innovation. It considers there is limited scope for growth in existing products or segments and it aims to have one new potentially major product in test each year.

Rowntree considers its competitive edge covers a number of factors:

Careful segmenting of the market with a strong emotional appeal to consumers.

Heavy emphasis on individual brands.

Keeping its existing products contemporary and reinforcing the consumers' emotional commitment.

The company also has a strong reputation for people concern and development going right back to Seebohm Rowntree, chairman in the 1920s and 1930s, and these attitudes persist. It seeks to select ambitious people with a strong desire to succeed and a readiness to be judged on performance against target. This concept has not been extended to remuneration, however.

For a company which has followed a strong brand philosophy, Rowntree does not appear to have quite the aggressive attitudes or people associated with this approach. The softer, traditional attitudes still prevail in the company.

The profitability is not dissimilar to Cadbury's and there is scope for improvement. Competition in the confectionery market will increase as will the power of multiple retailers to achieve special deals. Rowntree has a very distinctive brand approach to the market and what it considers to be the strong emotional values of its products compared with those of its competitors, but there are signs that competitors are adopting variations on this emotional appeal.

Both Rowntree and Cadbury are driving hard for growth in the US and in due course this could provide another interesting comparison of two quite different approaches to the market-place.

SOFT DRINKS

Schweppes   **Beecham Drinks**

The growing £1.5 billion soft-drinks business in the UK is unusual for a number of reasons. It has a concentrated-squash segment which is virtually unique to the UK and which has retarded the growth of pure fruit drinks compared to the way they have developed in other countries.

In the carbonated segment Coke and Pepsi have a much smaller share than in other markets, and other drinks like lemonade and certain proprietary flavours like Tizer have stubbornly retained customer loyalty against the invaders.

The third main segment covers mixers and this has traditionally been dominated by Schweppes.

Finally, there are health drinks such as Ribena and Lucozade and a variety of others which are made from concentrated syrup or from cubes or powder, such as Bovril and Horlicks.

The two major companies involved are Schweppes and Beecham. Both have their own products and they have the Pepsi and Coke franchises.

Jacob Schweppes started making artificial mineral waters in 1783 in Geneva, and in 1792 brought his unique system to London. Before the merger with Cadbury in 1969, Schweppes had extended its operations into Australia, the United States, South Africa, Europe and Africa. By acquisition it moved into concentrated fruit drinks with Kia-Oro and Roses' Lime Juice, and into foods, tea and coffee with Chivers, Hartley, Kenco and Typhoo. However, its mainstream activity remained in mixer soft drinks, a market it virtually owned. Its challenge is to build the Schweppes brand in other segments of the soft-drinks business in the UK.

Schweppes has a strong market orientation and just prior to the Cadbury merger had pioneered the major 1960s packaging innovation in the UK – the introduction of the single-trip glass bottle. The merger strengthened this orientation and subsequently even bolder strategies were developed, aimed at spreading the Schweppes brand strength in the UK and international soft-drinks markets, while retaining its heritage in the mixer business. In the early 1980s Schweppes began a major programme of market and product development.

The soft-drinks market is very competitive, with a large number of heavily supported brands. It is highly fragmented and the production process made it easy to enter on a regional and own-label basis. At the time there were many commodity type products like lemonade and cola, and developing a unique appeal was not easy. Young people were an important buying influence and there were various diet and health pressures on the market.

Schweppes carried out extensive research to understand needs, attitudes, preferences and buying habits in the market. It wanted to know what products and packaging were appropriate, and how competitive products were viewed, particularly by teenagers. Out of this consumer research and an international product-development programme came a range of staple flavours and new varieties for the

UK and overseas markets, packaged in the containers consumers and retailers preferred.

Schweppes is now firmly established in the non-mixer soft-drinks markets, has a major share of the large-plastic-bottle grocery market, is brand leader in canned soft drinks in grocery and off-licence outlets, and has established new flavours in a business which tends to stick to old faithfuls.

The imaginative advertising for which Schweppes is famous supported this market development, and already there are signs of emergent brand loyalty in the teenage market, not traditionally associated with Schweppes products.

This growth has also brought improved profit performance. Commitment to further development is clearly stated by Cadbury Schweppes' chief executive Dominic Cadbury: 'We are the custodians of one of the few great international brands and we never allow ourselves to forget that. In some two hundred years Schweppes came to own the mixer market. Now, we are well on the way to being a major force in the entire soft drinks market. That takes determined, committed management.' It has also demonstrated the effectiveness of one of the UK's few global marketing operations.

Beecham Drinks is part of the international Beecham Group. It has products ranging from prescription and proprietary medicines, veterinary products, toiletries, cosmetics, adhesives and household products to food and drink.

Its drink operations grew out of long-established Beecham products and from acquisition and franchising. The range is wide and includes standard carbonates, mixers, squashes, natural fruit juices and health drinks with brands like Corona, Hunts, Quosh, Sholer, PLJ, Ribena, Lucozade, Horlicks and Bovril.

The Beecham culture is strongly market-led with the emphasis firmly on brands and not on Beecham. The organization is structured to support the marketing operations and the chief executive and board orientation reinforces this. Traditionally, Beecham has been inclined to protect brands and minimize risks to them. It has also had the classic tendency to over-research. In recent years its stance and management structure have been changing to meet the much tougher market demands and conditions.

Beecham encourages innovation within brands. Market research is used to support such changes rather than for its own sake. It emphasizes niche marketing and brand extension, to anticipate and create new markets arising from the faster rate of change in life styles and from external pressures. Brand managers are expected to grow volume with good margins through premium pricing and by emphasizing factors other than price.

Beecham markets the same products in many forms and for different purposes, to maximize return on the brand. Concentrated Ribena in large bottles; in ready-to-drink cartons, cans and bottles; baby Ribena; Sparkling Ribena; Ribena mixed with other flavours – these are all examples of how a traditional brand can be extended dramatically. Lucozade has been expanded from the in-home invalid drink in a large bottle, to an outdoors sportsman's drink in a small wide-mouth bottle.

This philosophy of exploiting strongly promoted brands to the maximum has been highly successful, and has been evident in the Beecham acquisitions of companies with well-known but under-developed brands which could be given the Beecham treatment, rather than building completely new brands from scratch. This has been done very successfully with Horlicks and Bovril, and increasingly with Marmite.

In mixer drinks Hunts has been less successful in breaking the Schweppes stranglehold, but the battle is far from over.

This creative brand strategy is coupled with firm disciplines on the achievement of financial budgets, and extreme concern about being beaten to the mark by competitors. Competitors are constantly under scrutiny on products, facilities, approach to the market and likely reaction to Beecham moves.

The marketing department communicates information on competitors and changes in the market to R&D and manufacturing, through regular planning and review meetings aimed at maintaining or creating a Beecham brand advantage. The whole organization is committed to this aim.

Beecham demands high performance from a small number of high-calibre people, ready to take calculated risks and act fast. There is little formalized training. At Beecham people generally learn by doing.

The planning process is comprehensive. Objectives are defined clearly and expected to be achieved.

The Beecham board recently made some major changes. The reason given publicly was that the company needed younger, more dynamic management after a long period of continuous growth which may have caused some complacency. The company declared that it had failed to seize opportunities when they presented themselves and probably had not been as imaginative as it ought to have been.

Yet Beecham's record in the market-place suggests that it created opportunities rather than waited for them to present themselves. Moreover, it has set an example of what can be achieved by squeezing brands to new lengths and by imaginative approaches to established markets. The financial performance has also been far from unimpressive.

If the new chief executive, John Robb, and his management team are going to make dramatic improvements on what has happened over the last few years, Beecham is indeed heading for exciting times.

TOILETRIES

Beecham Toiletries   Johnson & Johnson

The toiletries business is international and highly competitive. Its consumers range from babies to geriatrics. Some of the world's most creative and aggressive marketing companies are heavily involved, and major movements in sales volume are not unusual as the markets are heavily influenced by emotional and fashion appeal.

Beecham and J&J are two of the leading companies, each with a number of exclusive and common products.

Beecham Toiletries developed in a similar way to its drinks business, through its own traditional products and by acquisition of companies with good brands which Beecham were convinced could be exploited. Some of its best-known brands are Silvikrin, Vosene, Brylcreem, Body Mist, Badedas, Calgon, Maclean's and Aquafresh.

The strong market orientation is subject to the same disciplines as in the rest of the group. The guiding doctrine is: get the marketing right and everything else comes right; get the marketing wrong and the problems come. Market research is critical in a business so influenced by emotion and life style. Both products and concepts are probed deeply, as are competitors' activities. More so than in other areas, there is a strong intuitive element in the interpretation and understanding of the psychological research, and creativity in ideas and products is encouraged.

The Beecham talent for niche marketing and brand stretching is very evident in toiletries, with Silvikrin shampoos, hairsprays, shaders, toners and dressings, and Badedas bath additives, soaps and deodorants, packaged in a multiplicity of containers. In 1985, for example, research that identified changes in consumer tastes and requirements prompted the reformulation and repackaging of Silvikrin shampoo, which achieved a sales growth of over 40%. Similar reformulation treatment of Silvikrin hairspray, shaders and toners resulted in equivalent sales increases. In the Body Mist range, the introduction of a non-perfumed variant helped the brand to consolidate its position as the most widely used women's antiperspirant deodorant. The introduction of Maclean's Sensitive Teeth Formula toothpaste supplied a market niche for people suffering from gum sensitivity. The White Willow variant of Badedas was launched and helped to produce a 17% improvement in sales. This level of rapid market response to market need is not unusual. Beecham expects to have to reformulate and repackage at frequent intervals.

To maintain sales movements of this extent, and to continuously identify niche and brand extension opportunities, calls for a particular kind of marketing talent which has been referred to as creative and streetwise. The kind of people possessing such qualities are quaintly termed intelligent barrow boys. As in other parts of Beecham, training is focused on the basics of the business. Talent is expected to come through by learning on the job, in the market-place, rather than through classroom sessions.

Managers responsible for new brand and line extensions know they must make a return early on and that they *must* achieve budgeted profitability and sales volumes. Failure to do so is seen as a personal failure. Beecham expects consistency in brand marketing. Control of brand strategy is invested at a very senior level to ensure that a competitive edge is maintained by doing whatever is necessary.

Johnson & Johnson developed from a strong health-care base in surgical dressings, through adhesive bandages and other medical products to its present wide range of consumer, professional and

45

pharmaceutical items. In toiletries it is best known for its baby-care, plasters, dental, feminine-hygiene and skin-care products, which extend into face creams, shampoos and conditioners.

The company lays great stress on its credo which sets the culture by which the business is run. At the top is the statement of the company's first responsibility, which is to meet the needs of all users of the J&J products and services in the most effective way possible. The credo goes on to state how the organization will be managed. It is, of course, a statement of the ideal. But setting sights high is itself part of the philosophy.

It is a vastly different culture from that of Beecham. The company claims it has an individual and effective market orientation, which aims at leadership of markets or market segments. It concentrates on 'special benefit' products as opposed to 'me too' products or manufactured differences. This emphasis on leadership and distinctive products gives pre-eminence to in-depth research of key markets. Competitors' strengths and weaknesses are similarly diagnosed. It also requires strongly creative product development and single-minded champions to force new products through, together with a remuneration system that encourages and rewards such entrepreneurial talent.

J&J has demonstrated considerable skill in a number of areas and particularly in its ability to tailor products to major market segments, and then dominate them. The best example is baby care, where its brand is almost generic. J&J's blanket support for the segment has demonstrated that effective marketing does not have to be flamboyant and overtly aggressive. Its move to extend the brand to young women reflected a similarly gentle but effective approach.

The company's emphasis on distinctive special-benefit products requires special talent in identifying segment opportunities. J&J recently demonstrated this ability by its moves into the forty-plus women's market through the aptly named Empathy range of skin- and hair-care products.

Key features of the J&J approach are deliberate, careful analysis of particular market segments, concentration on a few key areas and the subsequent development of strong, distinctive custom products. Once in the market, it consolidates and strengthens its position through product improvement and range extension, making it extremely difficult for competitors either to survive or come in.

Throughout J&J's consumer products business, over 30% of sales are in products introduced over the past five years. Given the strength of J&J products in their market segments, that is a rather unexpected statistic. The explanation is that, for J&J, new-product development is as important as holding on to existing market niches. Johnson & Johnson's approach to its market is individual, but it appears to be very effective. Certainly, the company appears to handle competition in its sectors with relative ease.

Even in design J&J has a distinctive style. Some would say it was rather old-fashioned; others would call it professional. It is certainly not avant garde. This style is deliberate. J&J considers it is worth using the best designers to achieve the best combination of convenience, suitability of function and visual appeal. Once agreed and tested in the market, a J&J design tends to last for a considerable time.

As in many other markets, own brands are major competitors. Supporting its brands and its special image against this threat is a major challenge for J&J – probably more so than combating other manufacturers' brands.

The J&J 'person' is also different. The company claims that he or she is well educated, ambitious, with strong personal values. Training is considered part of every manager's responsibility, rather than a centralized activity, and arises from personal appraisals where training needs are identified.

When asked the reason for J&J's continuing success, Bob Shire, the UK general manager, put it down to three factors: the company credo, decentralization and managing the business for the long term.

The J&J credo is so comprehensive and far reaching that it is difficult to see it as a meaningful guide to managing a major international company. In essence, the credo merely states the company's responsibilities to its customers, its employees, its communities and its stockholders, providing a general framework for operational decision-making. Nevertheless, it is clearly very important in J&J operations.

The credo starts with: 'We believe our first responsibility is to those who use our products and services.' J&J has demonstrated its talents at doing this both in a general marketing sense and by the swiftness of its reaction to consumer issues. In 1982, when Tylenol on Chicago store shelves was poisoned, it withdrew the product at a cost of $50 million. That reflects an unusual but truly impressive customer orientation.

FOOTWEAR

C. & J. Clark   **Hi-Tec Sports**

The footwear business has seen dramatic change in virtually every area of its operations: materials, manufacturing technology, products, distribution and marketing. Since the last war and particularly during the last twenty years the rate of change has accelerated significantly, as vertical and horizontal integration took place, and a few major groups came to control retail outlets and manufacturing facilities.

As life style changed, sport and leisure activity increased, fashion spread into men's and children's shoes and the business became much more fragmented. All these influences attracted foreign imports (now over half the market). Competition in the market intensified and presented opportunities for keen-sighted entrepreneurs to carve out their profitable niche business.

The two companies in the study represent the opposite extremes of the industry – Clark's with a 160-year history and a comprehensive product range, and Hi-Tec in its fifth full year, specializing in sports shoes.

The C.&J.Clark name is synonymous with footwear and has been in existence since 1825 when, after three years of making sheepskin rugs, the brothers Cyrus and James produced a pair of slippers called Brown Peters. Clarks were in the shoe business – and there they have remained, resisting temptations to diversify beyond what they know and understand.

Originally, Clark's shoemaking was a cottage industry with the factory assembling shoe components made by cottagers. In the 1850s a new, remarkable machine was invented which revolutionized the shoe industry and many others. It was the sewing machine, and it meant that shoes could be produced on an assembly line.

Between 1875 and 1940 Clark's multiplied its business eight times over and led the industry in technology and product development.

However, the explosive growth came between the 1950s and the 1970s when sales increased to over £600 million in a business employing some 23,000 people throughout the UK, Europe, North America and Australia, and producing seventeen million pairs of shoes a year.

Clark's manufactures, wholesales, retails and exports its products, competing successfully against a flood of inexpensive imports from the Far East and surviving where many others have failed. Market research indicates the Clark's brand name to be seven times stronger than its nearest competitor. Daniel Clark insists that maintaining the integrity of the brands is vitally important, 'because we want them to be here in fifty years' time'.

In 1981 Clarks acquired K Shoes, a company not much younger than itself and, like Clark's, involved in the manufacture, retailing and international marketing of shoes. Clark's is the largest shoe manufacturer in the UK and the second largest company in shoe retailing, where it owns Peter Lord, Bayne and Duckett, James Baker, The Clark's Shop, K Shops, John Farmer, Ravel and other well-known names in Europe, America and Australia.

Despite the fact that it is the second-largest shoe company in the world after Bata the company gives the impression of an almost genteel, slightly dull, small-town family business. Nothing could be further from the truth; it is a tough, market-driven, technologically advanced, financially stringent, aggressive organization. It has studied its markets in great depth, analysed social, fashion and life-style trends, and has utilized new materials, new concepts and new technology for the changing needs of its markets. Its concern about understanding customer needs goes back to the 1930s when it moved into retailing to learn first-hand about customers and also to create a market-place for its products.

Today, in a much more complex environment, managing director John Clothier considers this sophisticated probing of markets and competitors is even more critical. No longer are customers prepared to suffer agony for the first week of new shoes, as evidenced by the increasing popularity of moccasins, training shoes and casual business styles.

Clark's brought a different concept to children's shoes, placing enormous emphasis on foot health. Generations of children have grown up on Clark's shoes. More recently the company was faced with the problems of creating an equivalent appeal for the fashion-conscious teenage group. The Polyveldt casual was a strong move in that direction, and 'Levi's for feet' are aimed straight at the jeans generation.

Identifying the potential of upmarket fashion, Clarks took itself into the Ravel brand. This established chain of retail shops appeals to the fashionable young. Located in city centres alongside fashion-clothes retailers, the chain sources its merchandise from all over the world.

The company's progress faltered during 1978–81 when there was a strong production influence, with products and styles remaining virtually unchanged. As Clothier remarked, 'Come 1978, things were going very well indeed. We started to forget some of the key factors in our success formula. We didn't forget about quality or fit. But we did forget the style, and stopped innovating there.' The market drive has been re-established by placing emphasis on market segmentation and competitive advantage through innovation, style development and strong promotion and selling.

Clark's is clear on its market and financial objectives. These are tough, but the commitment to achieving them is fostered through the company's strong interest in its staff and in their training and development. It has built a reputation on knowing its business in depth, sticking to its last, producing consistent quality, innovative products and leading the market.

Clark's is very aware of the need for all areas of the business to operate effectively, but it is under no illusions that in the highly competitive markets in which it operates, the present and future of the organization are dependent on superior performance in the market-place. When that was forgotten at the end of the 1970s, the company paid the price and relearned the lesson that it had to be at least marketing led, and preferably market driven.

Hi-Tec provides a complete contrast to Clark's in every respect but marketing orientation. Founded in 1974 by its present chairman, Frank van Wezel, the company was known until 1982 as Inter-Footwear. It marketed the Inter brand sports shoes, and was linked with the parent Inter company in Holland. As a result of changes in the Dutch company, the decision was taken to split from Inter and establish Hi-Tec Sports Ltd, marketing the Hi-Tec brand.

Inter was strongly established at the budget end of the market and during the transition period it was essential to transfer the brand strength to Hi-Tec, with no loss of store listing because of the change. This was achieved during 1982 and 1983 in three distinct steps:

1 The introduction of Super Inter ranges to take the products up to the planned Hi-Tec level, but still using the Inter Footwear trading range.
2 The introduction of 'Hi-Tec by Inter' and the virtual dis-appearance of the Inter brand. This step established Hi-Tec as the listed brand with the Inter goodwill retained.
3 The Hi-Tec brand was quickly accepted by the trade as a first-class product, and at the end of 1983 the decision was taken to change the company name to Hi-Tec Sports Ltd.

Maintaining market position was the critical element in the changeover and final split, since the Dutch Inter company intended to come into the UK market with its own products, immediately the transition period was over.

The products of both companies were sourced from the Far East, but Hi-Tec had already established a research and development unit in Taiwan to improve quality, sharpen style and reposition the product line. This R&D unit was strengthened to support the plan for major expansion of the Hi-Tec brand.

In 1982 Hi-Tech's turnover was £7.5 million and pre-tax profits were £209,000. By 1985 it had increased turnover to £27 million and profit to nearly £2 million.

Not surprisingly, the board of Hi-Tec is strongly market oriented and although little formal research is commissioned the company keeps a close watch on the sports and leisure markets. It does this through monitoring publications, extensive travelling and store visits, detailed discussions with sports people, coaches, clubs, retailers and advertising agencies, and contact with the press. It also watches the developments and activities of competitors closely, particu-larly trends being established by the major international com-panies.

Hi-Tec has identified market segments that hold major growth opportunities. It has gone for product advantage based on leadership in style and cosmetic features, and upon a consistent, distinctive design theme running through all its ranges. Technology of sports-shoe manufacture is now widely known, so the competitive edge has to come from styling and quality of construction to ensure performance to the standard required.

Hi-Tec has majored on the squash market and sponsors the British open championship to encourage the sport and strengthen the relationship. It has also identified itself with well-known figures in other main sports and leisure activities, and now has a very comprehensive product range, which places it very close to the market leader.

Hi-Tec chief executive Terry Mackness lists the main features of the company's successful strategy:

Being better informed and wider awake than the competition.
Having the best product for money in the market.
Consistently providing the right colours and cosmetic appeal, as a result of projecting two years ahead.
Translating world trends into the UK market.
Being better than others at appropriating ideas.
Being creative and aggressive in the market-place.

In this tough business, the company has a management style reminiscent of US companies in the way it emphasizes performance and links rewards to achievement. It has grown fast and is set to achieve its objective of being number-one brand in the UK sports footwear market. The company has successfully established itself in the core sport and tournament segments and extended the brand into fashionable leisure wear. It positioned itself to exploit a market gap between an inactive Dunlop and an expensive Adidas, and has significantly increased its share of a growing market.

The move from sports footwear into associated bags and clothing is already taking place, and sports equipment is under review. The strategy will follow the same segment-by-segment exploitation, based on combining strong functional performance with fashion-conscious styling, and backed by heavy, imaginative promotion and links with well-known sports personalities.

Hi-Tec has read the market well and understands the implications of the changes in life style towards sports and leisure. It has managed to combine streetwise trading instincts with strategic marketing thinking, and has grown very quickly to number-two brand in the UK sports footwear market. With substantial growth objectives set for the next five years, the big challenge will be the move into the major international league.

Manufactured durables

CARS

Jaguar **BMW**

The luxury saloon-car market is dominated by the Jaguar, Mercedes and BMW marques, with a few other companies trying to find a way in. If these cars are analysed on style, performance or reliability it is clear that there are other, cheaper vehicles which could meet those needs perfectly adequately. Yet customers are not only prepared to pay high prices for Jaguars, Mercedes and BMWs but often demonstrate a remarkable loyalty to a particular marque, even when it is going through a bad patch.

In the UK the influence of company-owned cars is significant; however, there are other less tangible but very real factors which affect this particular market.

Jaguar cars go back to 1922, when Sir William Lyons founded the Swallow Sidecar Company to produce motorcycle sidecars. Five years later the production of car bodies started and in 1928 the company moved to Coventry. In 1935 the company came on to the London Stock Exchange and the name SS Jaguar appeared. Jaguar merged with the British Motor Corporation in 1966. BMC later joined with Leyland to form British Leyland, which was designed to create a bigger and stronger unit within the UK motor industry.

The 1975 implementation of the Ryder Report on BL led to operational difficulties and heavy Jaguar losses in 1979. The emphasis within BL was on quantity, not quality, and the very existence of strong subsidiary names was seen as a threat to corporate unity. Telephonists at the Jaguar plant were instructed to answer calls with 'Good morning, Leyland Cars'. If further identification were needed, the telephonist had to refer to 'large assembly plant number one'. The employees' pride in the product vanished overnight. Sir William Lyons returned briefly to remove his portrait from the boardroom. Only when the Jaguar identity was restored did he bring back the picture.

Jaguar Cars was re-created in 1980 under John Egan, as a separate organization within the BL Group. Two years later Jaguar Cars assumed responsibility for marketing and sales of its products in the US and Canada, which until then had been part of a central BL marketing set-up. By 1982 Jaguar was again profitable. In 1984 the decision was taken to float the company, and this was done success-fully in August of that year. After eighteen years Jaguar was back in the private sector. Its public experience will hopefully be a lesson in how not to run a company.

In John Egan's words: 'Jaguar's business is making money satisfy-ing customers', and to do this meant getting the product quality right after a period of continuous problems. It was also necessary to organize the distribution system. A thorough overhaul of the dealer network ensured that the cars were distributed and serviced by organ-izations that shared Jaguar's commitment to quality.

Having used the BL marketing and sales organization for many years (which has to be an interesting reflection on the market-place understanding of the people who structured a multiproduct business in that way) Jaguar had to establish a specialist team to match the worldwide skills of Mercedes and BMW.

To be fully effective also required a much deeper understanding of what motivated customers to buy this type of car; why they stuck to a particular marque; what the perception of Jaguar and its competitors was; how important were company hierarchy motives, and percep-tions of sportiness, individuality and beauty; how were dealers treating their customers, and whether the dealers were appropriate to the Jaguar type of business.

With a total commitment from the top and right through the organ-ization to re-establish Jaguar in the world's markets, the first priority was to get the quality right. While this was being achieved, Jaguar carried out a carefully planned communications programme to keep distributors, agents and customers informed about what was being done. Next priority was the development and launch of a new, care-fully researched range, handled by the smaller, high-calibre distribu-tion organization, motivated and supported by the Jaguar marketing and sales team.

To achieve the performance standards within the company and its distributors required a heavy investment in training and a new rela-tionship with suppliers, based on the need to meet Jaguar quality standards. Analysis of the causes of customer complaints showed that 60% of the 150 key areas of fault were caused by faulty components. Egan's answer was to involve the suppliers in resolving the problems, appointing their representatives to internal task forces so they could see for themselves the problems they caused. He also obliged them to agree to a contractual arrangement under which, if they exceed an agreed level of faults, they have to pay all the costs of putting it right – and that can be very expensive if the car is already in service. In 1984 the results came through strongly with increased sales in all major markets, a clear vindication of Jaguar's policy of providing well-designed, value for money cars, backed by the highest standards of customer service.

The rationalization and development of the distribution network reduced the total number of outlets but strengthened individual franchise holders and enabled them to provide the higher standards of after-sales care that Jaguar was demanding.

The comprehensive customer-tracking research (interviewing 100 customers each month on how well they are satisfied with both the vehicle and dealer service) also demonstrated growing customer approval of Jaguar products, and increasing levels of satisfaction with dealer sales and service.

In the UK, Jaguar increased its volume and its already dominant market share, despite a small fall in the total car market. Similar gains were achieved in the major international markets and with total turnover 34% up and profit more than 80% up over 1983, the foundations had been laid for solid growth.

During 1985 the strategy was fine-tuned to suit both the much-improved market standing and the buoyant demand for the current range, which had exceeded supply in most markets. This enabled the new model XJ40 to be subjected to the most exhaustive testing and probing programme ever undertaken. Jaguar claims it will set unmatched standards in its ride, handling, performance and economy, together with the high levels of quality, durability and reliability which research has indicated its customers demand.

The transformation in four years has certainly been spectacular, and if the market responds as expected to John Egan's beautiful new XJ40, the future could be equally impressive.

BMW operates in the same markets as Jaguar but with little of the latter's visual appeal in its products. It has a much wider range of vehicles, from the small 3 series to the very expensive 6, and it has the engineering standards expected of its country of origin. The BMW range sells very successfully all over the world and volume has increased consistently during this decade, as has the company's profitability. Within this increased total sales volume the top 6 and 7 series have maintained their level, the 5 series has started to decline, and the 3 series has had spectacular growth.

The reasons for the BMW success are more to do with creative marketing than enlightened engineering or manufacturing investment. The management of the company in Germany and the overseas companies has managed to create a total package with a high level of appeal – almost mystique – which is matched by few other products in any market.

This has been the outcome of very thorough analysis of what influences car buying; identifying particular segments and what is important to them; tracking social trends; knowing exactly what competitors are doing and how customers rate BMW against other marques. Since the product coming out of Germany is essentially the same, the appeal to particular markets has to be on the basis of this deep understanding of what is important.

The BMW competitive edge is multi-faceted and does not emphasize any single feature like high performance. Quality and reliability are projected in a taken-for-granted manner, as are efficiency and economy. Driving a BMW is fun. Buying a 3 series means you have joined the BMW club and are associated with the 6 series. The BMW driver is depicted as a discriminating, special individual.

BMW carefully segments its markets on specification, pricing, tax arrangements and company-car benchmarks. The BMW image is modern, quality, performance, status – it allows no aspect of weakness. Advertising features a range of appeals aimed at reinforcing a customer's motivation for buying a BMW in several ways simultaneously.

Paul Layzell, the UK managing director, makes the point very strongly that the BMW philosophy is built around customer satisfaction. The customer must be satisfied in the choice of car, when he is driving it and when he needs service support for it. Emotional reinforcement for the enlightened choice comes through follow-up contact and advertising. To achieve this wide-ranging support requires carefully selected and well-trained staff and dealers dedicated to the BMW approach to success. Ties with dealers are close and both they and BMW staff have performance-related incentives, in line with the company philosophy of covering every influence on customer satisfaction.

BMW only began its UK marketing activity in 1980, yet it has been outstandingly successful in its selected market segments. The small 3 series has achieved a very fashionable image and has almost cult appeal in the British market, with customers prepared to pay a very high price for the perceived benefits, image and status of the car. Similarly, at the other end of the range the UK is the second-largest foreign market for the large 6 series BMWs. In the total UK market, which fell by 2% in 1984, BMW achieved a 2% increase in its volume, and 1985 showed a further increase. The success of the marque is such that over 90% of the BMW dealers in the UK are happy to represent BMW exclusively.

The success of the BMW strategy throughout the world is an example of how a product which is unexceptional in any particular aspect can be made to appeal and sell to what are probably the most discriminating and difficult buyers. This is the result of carefully planned, imaginative and very clever marketing strategies which appear to be the antithesis of what is normally supposed to be the most effective approach. No single feature is claimed as the product's competitive edge. That lies in the total emotional appeal and satisfaction when the whole BMW package comes together.

HOME AND OFFICE

Black & Decker   3M

Some companies appear to be able to produce a stream of successful new products almost effortlessly. This is particularly noticeable in the home and office markets where there is a continuous interest in finding ways of doing things better or more easily. It is also an environment where market and product development virtually interchange and need to work more closely as partners than in most other businesses.

Among the successful companies in this new-product business

Black & Decker and 3M stand out for their consistent high performance.

Black & Decker founded its British subsidiary some sixty years ago and for most of that time was associated with power drills and their adaptations. Today it still has over 80% of the indoor power-tool market, but is also heavily involved in many other DIY products, in gardening equipment and more recently in small home appliances. It is strongly market driven, dedicated to growth primarily through product innovation and disciplined marketing, and targeted on making life easier for consumers, particularly in the leisure and DIY markets.

B&D in the UK is part of the European operations and less than 50% of the UK turnover comes from products manufactured in this country. Plants are highly automated under a strategy aimed at making B&D *the* low-cost producer. The parent-company strategy is to capitalize on the Black & Decker brand name and worldwide distribution, to emphasize new products both internally developed and acquired, and to globalize product offerings and manufacturing.

Maintaining a stream of consistently successful new products requires detailed understanding of what is important to particular market segments, what competitors are offering and how they are viewed by consumers. B&D traditionally kept its finger on the consumer pulse through guarantee-card registrations. The consistent 20% return provided immense and immediate information and established a very close and direct link between the company and its customers.

This extensive research confirmed the strength of the B&D name and showed the opportunities for cordless products and small home appliances. It has enabled B&D to sharply focus its marketing, giving it the discipline to minimize failure and ensure that – of the many new ideas which are encouraged internally and externally – only likely winners survive the formalized and prioritized new-product development system.

The disciplined approach also extends to sales policy, where the chief executive is directly involved in pricing, discounting and trading arrangements.

Like many other successful companies, B&D's strategy is essentially very simple. Making life easier for consumers provides almost limitless opportunities which the company seeks to satisfy through the development and marketing of new products from whatever source can provide them.

Innovation is critical to such a strategy. The highly successful paint stripper introduced in 1982 was basically a hair dryer, but it worked. The market opportunity and technology had been there for a long time, but B&D was the company that saw them. Like most of B&D's products, the stripper made a normally difficult job easier. The company hopes its mechanical weeder will do the same thing for an equally troublesome job in the garden.

B&D has a strong financial orientation to its marketing and a commitment to achieving results. It is essentially pragmatic in its attitude to products and policies, and is looking now to the next stage in the state of the distribution art. Computerized store provisioning will link manufacturer and retailer more closely and help to overcome what tends to be an almost adversarial relationship where both consider the ultimate customer as their direct responsibility.

The company is also identifying the opportunities which changing life styles and socio-economic environment will create over the next decade; what the next stream of innovative new products will have to be; and where they are likely to originate. The coming decade will see increasing DIY or shared DIY, and a change in the home environment towards more varied individual pursuits. This opens many new doors to imaginative, well-designed convenience products. B&D is enlarging its range of products and the scope of its operations.

B&D's markets will become increasingly competitive. The company believes its success will depend on knowing more than its competitors about what makes these markets tick, on having better antennae to identify segment opportunities, and on having the innovational talent to produce the unique or different products to satisfy those needs. The strength of the B&D brand will also play a significant role.

Communicating this philosophy throughout the organization and encouraging participation in the development of innovative thinking in products, manufacture and marketing is as central to the company as is the commitment to growth and achievement of results.

3M has been in the UK since 1929 and follows the basic strategies of its US parent, adapted to the British environment. The company is heavily oriented towards the market and chief executives like Bob

Olney tend to have a marketing background or have had major marketing experience. The 3M market orientation is clearly new product and technology driven. It aims to have, at any time, 25% of its business coming from products or services introduced within the previous five years.

The company is dedicated to the achievement of this objective and emphasizes that although the corporation owns the technology, it is available to everyone. Scientists are allowed and encouraged to spend 15% of their time on personal new-product development, and this is increasingly encouraged in other areas as well. The funding philosophy is to spread small amounts over many projects, and let natural selection identify those which are worth backing further.

The organization is also structured on a strong divisional emphasis, which spawns further departments and divisions as the market or new products make them desirable.

The emphasis on product creativity extends to researching the market in an effort to find what Bob Olney terms 3M's 'unfair advantage'. The company places a strong emphasis on finding an edge in a market segment or niche, exploiting it in an imaginative way, and then introducing further products to the segment. One good video tape is much the same as another, but 3M consumer research showed that there was concern over how long tapes would wear. To overcome this, 3M introduced its lifetime guarantee (which competitors could also have done). In doing so, it removed the concern and increased its market share from 8% to 20%.

Doing things differently and better is encouraged and the company places major emphasis on enterprise and excellence. Mistakes and failures are accepted as an inevitable part of the system, and even they are examined creatively. The ubiquitous 'Post it' notes were the result of research into a permanent adhesive which produced an unusual spin-off product: it stuck when needed and could be removed without leaving a mark. Now 3M charges a high premium price for what are special-effect sticky labels. Customers pay the premium because the product is so convenient to use.

3M also considers that as more and more business comes from fewer and fewer customers, it is important to build on its existing customer base by riding new products in on the back of existing ones, and a strong corporate identity helps it to do so.

The company takes a characteristically innovative view of globalization and uses it or not as it considers appropriate in particular national markets. It also emphasizes quality, which it defines as 'providing customers with what they expected to get'. It believes that driving up quality drives down costs, and that this applies to products, marketing and administration.

It is also very aware of the changing market-place in terms of customer size, government influence, retailer muscle and consumer life styles; and it responds in an essentially pragmatic way by emphasizing what works in the particular environment. It acknowledges that new products need to be plentiful, regular, and introduced quickly and effectively.

3M has a number of basic strategies. It believes that high market share is important because it tends to be associated with high profit, particularly when linked to a low-cost producer strategy. It also follows a market segmentation and niche strategy majoring on its unique strengths in product development.

The company has a very clearly defined mission to build businesses. It has created a culture which stimulates creativity in technology, products and ideas, yet ensures that this creativity is always oriented to the market-place and the development of new profitable businesses. It rewards success in effective, emotionally satisfying ways, since it considers remuneration is already high – through awards, by publicizing success, and by encouraging initiative and responsibility. It also supports people whose products fail and encourages them to be successful next time around – the reverse of the traditional company, where the failed innovator receives only ignominy.

3M spends over 6% of turnover on research, and believes in creating many new products, accepting that the good ones will win through and that the fall-out rate will be high at the low-investment stage.

There is little doubt that 3M has few equals in developing products and building businesses. It has managed to combine a deep understanding of markets, competitors, technology and manufacturing, which produces a consistent supply of successful new products and services.

Pervading the company is a climate which encourages employees to find new and better ways of doing things, by assuring them of 3M's willingness to take risks, to support innovative ideas and to recognize that not all new efforts will succeed.

It believes that the company's financial and technical strengths have been created by innovators and that these company strengths are resources which innovators can draw on to build the businesses of tomorrow.

Black & Decker and 3M have very similar corporate philosophies and already they are starting to fish in the same DIY pond. If they pursue their stated missions the leisure market could see a very interesting battle develop between two of the world's most successful and pragmatic new-product marketing companies.

PORTABLE POWER

Ever Ready   **Duracell**

The battery business in the UK goes back some sixty years. The Ever Ready company dominated it until the early 1980s. Growth until the 1950s was unspectacular, but with the arrival of the smaller transistor radios, demand increased dramatically and by 1977 sales volume in the UK was 471 million, valued at almost £90 million, with radios taking about half of the market. Of the remaining volume only torches had a double-figure share, followed by toys, calculators, cassette players, shavers, cameras, radio/cassette players and clocks.

In 1977, almost all the batteries used were the traditional zinc carbon cells, but an almost unknown alkaline type had its toe in the water with about 1%. Ever Ready had some three-quarters of a market which was never going to be the same again.

The Ever Ready company was developed by a strong, driving chairman until the 1950s, and thereafter its dominance in a fast-developing market was almost a licence to print money. Perhaps not surprisingly, emphasis changed from creating growth to managing it, with a different style of management, more interested in avoiding mistakes than developing new markets.

During the Second World War, Ever Ready had a quarter share in Mallory Europe Ltd which was established to produce button-cell batteries. After the war alkaline battery development was carried on by this company, which was seen as Mallory rather than Ever Ready. During the mid-1970s the battery business was looked at by the Monopolies Commission and in 1977 Ever Ready decided to sell its share of Mallory. At that time, with some 75% of a market which was about 99% zinc carbon, with a highly profitable business and with a conservative management, the Ever Ready decision was supported by a company technical assessment, which tended to suggest that alkaline batteries were an American gimmick.

The decision to follow a defensive strategy and try to hold zinc carbon against the upstart alkaline was scarcely surprising. An offensive strategy, aimed at stimulating alkaline, would have meant heavy investment and a short-term profit decline. Unfortunately, the technical assessment was badly wrong. Ever Ready found itself with a large share of a declining market and no presence in the growing one, which started to develop very fast. By 1980 the alkaline battery had increased its market share to some 20% by value. Not content with shooting itself in the foot once, the Ever Ready management did it again by discarding its universal brand name in favour of the colourless Berec.

That year Ever Ready started to develop its own alkaline battery and tried to find a non me-too product, but without much success. In 1982, after the Hanson Trust takeover, the new management asked basic questions and developed a new market strategy based on extensive market research and technical assessment of the findings. Hanson also restored the traditional brand name, helping to restore confidence not just in the market but also among the employees.

The new alkaline batteries had a working life many times greater than zinc carbon, cost at least twice the price, and had a longer 'not in use' life. The zinc carbon type was not suitable for long continuous use because of chemical failure, but in many applications the use was not continuous and in these cases it was better value for money than alkaline. Coming between the two was the zinc chloride type which did not suffer chemical failure, had double the zinc carbon life, and at around 40% dearer was probably the best all-round value for money. Ever Ready also had assets and strengths in zinc production.

Given this strategic analysis, in 1982–3 the company decided to invest in alkaline and zinc chloride production, and to accept that this would depress zinc carbon business. Based on the detailed research, Ever Ready carefully segmented the market, positioning the three product types to give maximum advantage. It also carried out a range reduction.

Ambitious market-share objectives were set for both alkaline and zinc chloride, backed by heavy promotion, merchandising and aggressive selling. Manufacturing productivity was improved dramatically to reduce the manufacturing cost base, the management structure was streamlined and performance-related remuneration packages developed to stimulate commitment to the clear objectives which had been established to support the market-place goals.

In the battery business brand trust is critical; as ER marketing director Peter Bonner aptly says: 'Selling a battery is selling a promise.' Probing awareness, acceptance and loyalty of the Ever Ready against competitors was therefore vitally important. Research found the brand name to be still very strong despite the reduced market share and competitor promotions.

Ever Ready moved effectively to adapt to the major market changes. It halted the fall in its market share, initiated research-based product innovation, and developed aggressive marketing strategies to re-establish its dominant place. In 1985 its profit was double the 1983 level with its market share again well over 50% and growing. It had gone through the difficult re-orientation phase and was well placed in the growth segments of a market worth nearly £180 million.

It had developed an attacking strategy for its new products, to complement its skill at defending traditional business and had given itself a competitive edge by making good use of assets which the company had started to consider as obsolescent. It also had a board convinced by results that its market shaped its business.

When Ever Ready decided to sell its share in Mallory in 1977 it left a market wide open for the US partner Duracell to exploit. Duracell did so with considerable skill and single-mindedness, with none of the conflict of interest which faced ER since it had no zinc carbon investment to protect.

It followed the simple strategy which had been so successful in North America:

Concentrate on alkaline batteries.
Have a distinctive product appearance to make it clearly different.
Major on the fact that it lasts much longer.

The company brought in new European management experienced in fast-moving consumer-goods marketing, selected the distribution channels and outlets, and sold in and out hard, with strong merchandising support. It went after its major but weakly market-oriented competitor, and took full advantage of all the odds in its favour. It researched the market in depth, pinpointing its competitor's strengths and weaknesses. Then it used its international connections for product research and development to choose its battleground and weapons to take Ever Ready apart.

In a very short time it established its copper top-battery as different, technically superior and better value for money. It had nothing to lose in its existing business (the conflict Ever Ready had to face), and it had the alkaline market all to itself.

Duracell has moved fast and comprehensively in the UK market, but it seems to have been surprised at the effectiveness of the Ever Ready response once it put its house in order. The volume market share for alkaline has not grown as fast as anticipated and the changing end-use pattern for batteries is placing less emphasis on continuous running which is the strength of Duracell. It would not be the first occasion a traditional product has fought back on technical improvement and product innovation to slow the advance of a new-technology competitor.

Duracell has shown it can perform when most of the chips were stacked in its favour. It has organized itself well with lean, simple marketing strategies and objectives, very competent people managing the business, sound financial controls and planning that pays attention to detail. It claims Duracell people have proven backgrounds, good track records, like to run with the ball, are prepared to take risks and are achievement-oriented. They are encouraged by performance-linked remuneration and have freedom to operate.

The UK battery business could be in for a very fascinating period of highly aggressive competition.

COMPUTERS

IBM   **ICL**

The information technology business is one of a handful that impact on and across industrial, commercial, educational and social life and national boundaries. Like finance, entertainment and travel it is truly international and faces particular pressures – political, security, legal, personal and health. It is also one of the most complex and competitive markets, demanding high R&D investment, technological innovation, manufacturing excellence, firm financial disciplines and strong, aggressive marketing.

The rates of growth and technological change mean there is continuous scope for innovation, and opportunities abound for enterprising companies to start up with new product concepts or by finding solutions for the problems in particular market segments.

In the UK the output of the information technology industry is increasing at a compound growth rate of more than 12%, investment is rising and new markets are opening up. Despite the buoyancy, the UK industry is not meeting market demand and its growth rate is far less than that of the IT industry worldwide.

In this extraordinary business, IBM has been consistently successful, while ICL has had to fight its way through severe market and corporate difficulties and is now coming back as a major innovative force in the industry. Comparing the approaches of these two companies to what must be one of the supremely competitive markets provides an insight on what really affects success in such environments.

IBM was established over seventy years ago (in the UK half as long ago) and has successfully lived through all the dramatic change which has affected its industry. Its founder, Thomas J. Watson, articulated three simple commitments:

Respect for the individual. People are the company's greatest asset.
Service to the customer. Every employee's job relates to enhancing that goal.
Pursuit of excellence as a way of life. Sharpened by competition and reward into superior performance in both product and service.

These are still the basic beliefs of the company but they have been given a sharper edge by the addition of very specific business goals:

To grow as fast as the industry.
To maintain technological and product leadership.
To be the most efficient high-volume, low-cost, quality producer, marketer and administrator.
To generate sufficient profit to sustain growth.

IBM lives by these beliefs and objectives. But when the chips are down some are more critical than others. The most critical is service to the customer and throughout IBM the message is made clear: 'Remember, the customer pays your salary.'

The company is blatantly market-driven and led by executives who are committed marketing people. Markets are extensively researched, analysed, segmented and projected in a very basic, meaningful way. The information is important only for what it can do to give IBM a competitive edge, develop a new market or exploit an existing one more effectively, trigger a new product or improve an existing one. It stimulates organizational changes to match the specific needs of clearly defined market segments, and new ones capable of being developed. It reinforces the importance of the whole organization understanding how customers view their own business and how IBM impacts on it.

To be effective in the IT business large organizations have to be flexible and capable of competing with smaller companies which provide specialist expertise and attention in particular segments or niches. IBM's strategy had been to create independent business units containing specialist skills and solutions – for example in the academic and scientific communities.

The concern for customer service and excellence in all IBM operations places critical importance on the selection, development and motivation of its people. Training is central to both service and excellence, and involves skill development and manpower planning on a continuous basis. Its employees are expected to spend fully 5% of their time in training activities. IBM also insists on training for its dealers, to help them to achieve the high standards it considers essential. It also focuses on training for customers, to ensure they make the most effective use of the equipment and systems. In its recruitment, IBM looks for self-starters who can communicate and who will develop such talents through regular training and career enhancement moves. It also communicates its objectives very clearly, expects them to be achieved and rewards performance.

It is, quite simply, a strongly market-driven, well-managed organization which knows exactly where it intends to go and how it will get there – a formidable combination with a high likelihood of success.

The clear market orientation of IBM UK was very evident under the leadership of Sir Edwin Nixon, and the strong UK and international marketing pedigree of the current chief executive, Tony Cleaver, will reinforce the market emphasis in future IBM strategy. It will certainly be essential if IBM is to beat the tough new competition it is now facing.

ICL has had a much more chequered history and resulted from a series of mergers during the 1960s. In the 1970s the company achieved rates of growth well above the average in an industry renowned for rapid expansion. By the end of 1979 the fixed cost base had increased significantly as a result of overmanning exacerbated by the high UK inflation. At the same time the strength of sterling eroded ICL's competitive position in world markets. Like many other businesses which had grown fat in the 1970s, ICL was ill prepared to react swiftly in 1980 when severe recession in the UK brought a sudden halt in its business growth.

The sharp reversal in ICL's fortunes, the heavy resultant operating losses and a mounting debt burden made support from the government essential for the continued existence of the company. Support also gave ICL breathing space to take the radical measures necessary to put the company back on the road to recovery. The primary task was to restore ICL to profitability as an independent company. This involved major manpower reductions, significant organization changes to adapt to the needs of the changed business situation, and other cost-cutting and rationalization measures to reduce the cost base.

This fundamental reassessment of all aspects of the business led primarily to a new approach to marketing and product strategies, including collaborative ventures with other companies. The main organizational changes were:

The establishment of a new product marketing division to increase emphasis on the formulation and implementation of marketing strategies.

The creation of a strong team to develop standard applications software to increase the sales of ICL products to new customers.

The creation of separate development divisions for distributed systems, mainframe computers and networking strategy.

The new top management came from successful market-oriented

companies and brought similar personal strengths and international experience.

To give a clear, unified direction and set of objectives, the 'ICL Way' was promulgated. This articulates the ICL attitude to business and people, and spells out commitments to change, to customers, to excellence, to teamwork, to achievement and to people development.

Within this corporate philosophy, the present chairman and managing director, Peter Bonfield, who joined ICL in 1981 to lead the company's marketing operations, describes the ICL mission as 'supplying information systems to improve operating efficiency of clients in the international market-place'. To Bonfield, market penetration means profitability. To achieve it, ICL provides a total customer package including software support and what he terms 'intellectual value-added', rather than technical, input.

Bonfield believes that fast reaction to market change and readiness to work with others are critical differences between the previous and present ICL operations. Marketing orientation has replaced the narrower sales orientation and has involved heavy training programmes, selection of new people, personalized incentive schemes, small business units and extensive research into markets and competition.

He considers that innovative thinking in market and product development is critical to the company's survival. The company stresses fundamental research into basics such as who influences purchasing decisions and who uses the equipment, selecting limited market segments and exploiting those areas where ICL has a competitive edge, such as open networks and the 'one per desk' concept.

With manufacturing cost differences relatively small in efficient plants, flexible manufacturing to match market changes is more important than minimum cost. It is a reflection on the depth of commitment to making ICL one of Britain's most effective international companies that it has invested several million pounds in a huge executive retraining programme using experts from the UK, US and France. Board members and senior executives participate in this intensive marketing and management training, indicating just how important ICL considers this activity.

Says Bonfield: 'We needed to change our marketing approach radically, once and for all. An investment of time, money and effort on this scale was the only way to make the changes stick.'

The change in ICL's fortunes during the past three years has been substantial, although return on sales has not reached the 1979 ICL level nor the current level of IBM. However it has improved fast from the low point in 1981 and there is complete commitment within the company to make sure that progress will continue at an equally fast rate. Bonfield sees the critical elements of the new marketing oriented approach as:

Setting a clear vision of where the company is going.
Specialization in objectives and markets.
Working strategically with suppliers.
Communication throughout the whole organization and to customers.
Commitment to achieving objectives.

There are striking similarities between the IBM approach to the business and the new one being developed in ICL. It will be interesting to see how they maintain their respective competitive differences.

MECHANICAL HANDLING EQUIPMENT

JCB   **Lansing**

The markets for the construction equipment of JCB and the materials-handling equipment of Lansing are similar in character. They service customers to whom their products are supportive rather than mainstream; the business covers a range of industries; the markets are international and so is the competition.

Both companies are family owned businesses which have been built into major international forces in their particular industries, and both have come through the recession successfully and are competing effectively in international markets against the world's best.

JCB, the initials of Joe Cyril Bamford, who founded the business some forty years ago, is an unusual company. Now managed by chairman Anthony Bamford, the son of the founder, with Gilbert Johnston as chief executive, it has its headquarters in a landscaped site in a Staffordshire village, and has managed to stay remarkably profitable when most other construction equipment companies have gone into losses. It is debt-free and, in 1985, its capital spending amounted to some £16 million. Manufacturing plants are highly automated computer-controlled operations and about 10% of staff are employed in R&D, supported by an investment amounting to 5% of sales.

Its sales in 1985 were around £185 million with pre-tax profits of some £25 million. One product accounts for 70% of sales and the company competes against multinational giants from the US and Japan, with some 70% of its output going overseas.

JCB has been consistently successful apart from in 1980 when, battered by the recession, profits fell to £300,000. This stimulated the company to cut its workforce by a third and launch a major capital investment programme, to achieve a far-reaching modernization of its main Staffordshire plant. Since then the company has made itself efficient in manufacturing and increased the effectiveness of its management overall. But it has also established certain basic attitudes and a company culture that influences the whole way it does business, and which makes it distinctive in its market place.

In Anthony Bamford's words: 'Our strength is product intensity, knowing our market and concentrating on it.' It has clearly defined objectives:

To dominate its specific markets.
To concentrate on specific activities and not be sidetracked.
To be aware of both user and owner needs for construction equipment.

JCB researches its markets, customers and competitors to a depth that many fast-moving consumer goods companies would envy. It takes competitors' products apart, examines their strengths and weaknesses, assesses manufacturing costs and compares customer attitudes vis-à-vis its own and competitive products. The conclusions of this research are reviewed by multi-disciplinary teams composed of marketing, engineering, design and finance. They have one aim – producing a competitive edge for JCB products. Among the customer benefits they look for are flexibility, reliability, cost and ease of operation. This detailed knowledge also allows fast reaction to opportunities and the ready creation of new ones.

The product groups are intended to concentrate the talents and skills of the different disciplines on making the JCB product different and better than its competitors'. They also recognize that the product must sell profitably in a market where prices are at 1979 levels.

The company culture is highly competitive and single-minded, dedicated to the aggressive selling of JCB products. Employees are aware of the company as something special and different. The company chooses its people carefully and demands high performance and commitment from them.

Gilbert Johnston considers that JCB makes its own luck. He believes the reason why more competitors have not come into the key JCB backhoe-loader business is not just the competition's lack of domestic market penetration and the current world market saturation. It is equally a matter of continual innovation to keep ahead of the game, he declares.

JCB has demonstrated its ability to design and develop new money-making products and to beat competitors with its existing ones. It has established itself in the tough US market and taken everything the international giants have thrown at it. It is looking at new markets in the Far East, with China a prime target, and is preparing to face foreign competitors setting up manufacturing plants in this country.

The firm has a lean, very cost-effective business, which is essential for the highly competitive markets in which it operates. It knows its markets, its customers and its competitors better than they probably know themselves. It works hard to develop products superior to those of the competition, sells them aggressively and services them thereafter. It has concentrated on making its strengths stronger, eliminating its weakneses and doing what it is good at. This has been a very successful recipe so far.

Lansing Bagnall was founded in 1937 to make industrial trucks and tractors based on designs of the Lansing Company of Michigan. However, the market was not quite ready at that time. The company was acquired in 1943 by the present chairman, Emmanuel Kaye, who was convinced there would be a big post-war demand for materials-handling equipment and amalgamated the company with his own firm of precision engineers.

Through design expertise, engineering and marketing skills and mergers with Henley Forklift International and Bonser Engineering, Lansing Bagnall gradually put itself on the world map, with major interests in the manufacturing of industrial trucks as Lansing Henley, and in specialist machines and equipment for horticulture through Bonser Engineering. The marketing of both types of products later became the responsibility of Lansing Ltd.

The mission of the company is twofold: to be the best in the industry and to advance its position as the largest industrial truck company in the UK and as a major force internationally. To achieve this, Lansing concentrates its attention on customers, products, innovation, people and profit. The organization is tailored to meet market needs, with the joint managing directors and the rest of the board dedicated to customer satisfaction and cost consciousness.

In style Lansing is reminiscent of the better US companies that manage their affairs in a considered, deliberate way, leaving little if anything to chance. The equipment demonstration area would do credit to many fashion-oriented consumer-goods businesses, as would the almost balletic presentation of the products. Closeness to customers is central to the Lansing culture. The product demonstration facilities underline the thoroughness of its approach, as does the emphasis placed on bringing customers, industry bodies and suppliers to actually see for themselves the degree of detail which Lansing puts into customer understanding and service. The all-important personal contact is supported by quantitative and qualitative research into markets and competitors – all aimed at enabling the company to develop better products with an edge over the competitor.

The recession forced Lansing to tighten up its manufacturing operations, and like JCB it has not only streamlined and automated but has striven to make its investment in advanced technology also provide better products with greater added value, which can be translated into market share or margin gains.

Lansing considers it has one of the widest ranges of equipment in the world. It claims it has the right machine for any job, whatever the location, and that its products are ultra-reliable, backed by service facilities that span the globe.

Components are designed and manufactured in Lansing factories. This not only ensures fit and function to precise standards but also secures the lucrative replacement business.

Lansing believes it provides 'Total Involvement' through technical advice to match machines to problems, through training customers' personnel and through regular service inspections. This degree of service, which starts at the beginning and never stops, combines with machines tailored to specific market segments to form the Lansing competitive edge.

Lansing spells out its objectives clearly along with the reasons why achievement of them is critical. The company attempts to combine the accountability, flexibility and freedom of a small company with the strengths and stability of a large organization. This philosophy, with the strategic planning and commitment to success which is apparent in the company, has enabled Lansing to develop into a successful international organization, able to compete against major multinational competitors and come through the recession of the early 1980s which killed many other companies.

The company has achieved its growth and profitability through flexibility, concentration on business fundamentals – customers, products, people, profit – and a dedication to being better than its competitor. Despite its size it has retained the closeness and personal commitment normally associated with small businesses.

The similarities between JCB and Lansing are much greater than appear at first sight, and may well explain why both companies have been able to prosper in highly competitive international markets.

PART TWO

THE COMMON DENOMINATORS

The first part of this book summarized how twenty-eight companies had been successful in tough, competitive businesses. On the surface there appear to be as many differences in approach as there are similarities. Tactically that is true, and anything else would have been very surprising. But at the strategic level and in the whole culture of the companies, the common features are so apparent and so obviously influential in their success that only some human perversity or blindness must prevent their adoption by the majority of other companies who are struggling to succeed.

The ten market commandments are as basic to business success as the original ten commandments were to civilized social development. Hopefully the profit motive will make the implementation of the former more effective than the latter.

In no particular order the ten are:

1. Acceptance by the chief executive of the organization that customers are the ultimate determinant of its success or failure.
2. Having a clearly defined mission and set of objectives which are understood and accepted throughout the organization.
3. Having a deep understanding, as opposed to simply a knowledge, of what influences the environment and markets in which the company operates.
4. Assessing honestly the positive and negative assets of the company.
5. Identifying the particular segments or niches where real opportunities exist for the company.

6 Knowing the direct and indirect competition, what makes it tick and how it is likely to act and react.

7 Establishing the competitive edge which will make customers choose the products or services against those of the competition.

8 Bringing an open-minded perception to interpreting, developing and presenting the product, and the facilities and organization to support it.

9 Marketenvolk – selection, training and motivation of performers.

10 Total dedication to the achievement of corporate success in the market-place and of overall company objectives.

Chief executive commitment

In any company the chief executive influences what the culture will be. The culture is like the image of an organization; you cannot not have one. The question is, what kind of culture the company will have.

In most of the companies in the study, the CEO had influenced the culture of the business in a very positive way towards the marketplace and customer satisfaction.

In British Airways, Colin Marshall identified the earlier operations orientation as a main reason for the company's declining fortunes, not because operations were not critically important, but because they should respond to market needs rather than be the prime influence on the strategy of the company. In stomping around the airline's operations he reiterates one theme continuously – that it is the customer who pays everyone's salary. He also becomes personally involved in marketing decisions to the extent that they are automatically associated with his influence. Such was the case, for example, with one of the first marketing initiatives: Supershuttle. When British Midland began to snatch market share by offering passengers a hot meal on domestic flights, Marshall refused to be panicked into doing likewise. Instead, BA initiated market research into what people really wanted on such short trips. The research showed that customers now took for granted that they would be guaranteed a seat without making reservations; but it found that the only hot meal they wanted was breakfast. BA gave them what they wanted and swiftly restored the competitive status quo. While not a showman, Marshall is always on hand and in the thick of the launch of any significant marketing initiative, to demonstrate to customers and staff that he is firmly behind it. At British Caldedonian, too, the strong customer orientation was the reason for its survival.

Saatchi & Saatchi learned very early what should not have been necessary for an organization advising clients about influencing customers, namely 'the supremacy of the client', as joint managing director Terry Bannister terms it. However, deeply instilled in the S&S

culture now is that an advertising campaign is only good if it helps to achieve the client's marketing objectives. Ogilvy & Mather's main purpose is to serve its clients more effectively than any other agency. These are not just words. Top management expends considerable time and effort convincing other people in the organization that this is critically important to the success of the business.

Similar attitudes exist with Hertz and Avis, which comes as no surprise in such a customer-service oriented business. However, within the very different traditions of the banking and financial worlds, it was impressive to find the very high degree of market-place commitment demonstrated by the TSB's chief general manager Leslie Priestley, who considered himself a banker. With Abbey National, the orientation under solicitor Clive Thornton's leadership was high-profile publicity, developed to a more disciplined market awareness by Peter Birch with his extensive consumer goods marketing and general management experience.

In Bird's Eye and Smith's Crisps, we have two examples of market leaders who either misread or did not read their changing customer environment, and paid the penalty. In each case, recovery in company fortunes stemmed from a new chief executive re-establishing a basic customer-oriented strategy. Superficially it appears very surprising that two such companies should have ignored or not been aware of fundamental shifts in their markets; but it would seem that companies with a dominant market position arising from some over-whelming strength tend to concentrate attention on non-market elements of the business. As a result, they attract chief executives whose orientation is similarly away from the market.

The same mistakes were made in Ever Ready, for reasons similar to Bird's Eye and Smith's, and a major influence in recovery was again the return to customer orientation.

It is worth stressing here that leadership on its own is not enough to hold a company on the road to sustained profitability. In today's business environment the corporate leader who is not also a marketer can take his company very efficiently down any of a thousand side roads to disaster. Both he and his dedicated management team may be absolutely convinced they are heading in the right direction.

If we look at what happened to the companies in *In Search of Excellence* who lost their 'excellence' status, one factor stands out as common to all – they lost their closeness to their customers. The blame for this failure must rest with top management, whose job it is to ensure that the commitment to the company's chosen markets never wavers. In essence, one can say with considerable justification that you cannot have effective business leadership without a strong market orientation and that you cannot have a strong market orientation without leaders devoted to the marketing approach. There is no either/or – they are inextricably intertwined.

In the other consumer-goods companies competition was intense and generally the chief executive either came from a customer-oriented function or developed such an attitude because he considered it essential. But even in Cadbury's and Clark's, specific problems had arisen when this basic customer truth was ignored or neglected.

In Ever Ready the situation was similar to that of companies in other mature industries (like glass containers) which are highly capital intensive. Although the glass-container manufacturers were aware of changing customer preferences towards plastic packaging, they were reluctant to acknowledge the change because of the financial implications for their existing business. Such reluctance ultimately lets competitors come in to erode away customer loyalty and market share. The company then has the worst of all worlds – declining profits without compensating growth in other products. It happened in Ever Ready just as it happened in packaging and chemicals and numerous other industries. These same fundamental errors will continue to occur, until companies accept that it is customers – not the extent of capital investment a company makes – who determine what is purchased. Indeed, the greater the capital investment, the greater the need to be close to the customers.

In ICL, the same basic problems existed in a different guise. Sales orientation had become confused with customer orientation and major efforts were going into trying to sell products which customers did not wish to buy. The change of emphasis to the market-place very quickly highlighted the need for a new marketing rather than a selling strategy.

The other side of the coin is seen in companies like Beecham, Johnson & Johnson, Black & Decker and 3M, where not only chief executives but research, development and manufacturing directors see customer considerations as the major element in the philosophy of the whole company.

Perhaps the most impressive companies for customer awareness were JCB and Lansing, not because they were more oriented that way than the others, but because it was much less expected. In both cases they were facing intense international competition. Despite their strong engineering commitment there was a level of customer and general market orientation among chief executives and other board members which would have done credit to fast-moving consumer-goods companies.

It is interesting that some building companies are moving strongly in this same direction, changing from trying to sell something to a customer to much greater consideration of what the customer wants, e.g. sheltered housing.

The other significant feature of the chief executives in the companies studied was the variety of their backgrounds and experience. They had come up through marketing, sales engineering, accounting, banking, advertising, engineering research, flying and shipping; but they had all become aware of the overriding importance of customers and the market-place, either because they had moved into marketing or selling or because, by the time they had become responsible for the total business, they realized where the prime influence lay.

The significance of the chief executive orientation has been underlined by other research which has been carried out over the past few years. It appears to show a correlation between the major area of chief executives' experience and whether their companies are good at marketing, are market oriented or use basic marketing disciplines. The various surveys put the proportion of marketing-conscious firms at only between 30% and 40% of the total. More encouraging, however, is the growing acceptance by chief executives of the growing need to become more market oriented.

Why is there such a prevalent lack of customer orientation among British chief executives? At least part of the answer stems from a social and educational culture which views the competitive operation as a stressful activity to be avoided. This attitude also stems from the time when the British lead in manufacturing instigated a period of minimal competition. It was reinforced by the captive market of the empire and is taking a long time to fade away. Certainly the degree of devastation in many British industries caused by international competition can only be explained by a failure to understand the changing market and customer environments and to adapt business strategies to new situations.

Crunch highlights

The most successful chief executives have a market-place orientation and commitment.

This is an attitude of mind, not the result of a particular background or discipline.

It is essential whether the business is consumer, industrial or service.

Clearly defined objectives

Although described in different ways, all the companies in the study had clear strategies and very specific objectives.

They recognized that to capture and hold markets they need a vision of the future that will be understood and endorsed by all decision-makers in their organizations. The process starts, once again, with top management identifying the basic mission of the company – what it is in business for.

This is how US management guru Warren Bennis recently described the corporate mission statement:

> What is a vision? A vision should state what the future of the organisation will be like. It should engage our hearts and our spirits; it is an assertion about what we and our colleagues want to create. It is something worth going for; it provides meaning to the people in the organisation, in the work that they are doing. By its definition, a vision is a little cloudy and grand; if it were clear, it wouldn't be a vision. It is a living document that can always be added to; it is a starting place to get more and more levels of specificity.
>
> Now beyond that, when the vision statement is close to completion, the questions that also have to be asked in any organisation are: 'What is unique about us? What values are true priorities for the next era? What would make me personally commit my mind and heart to this vision over the next ten years? What does the world really need that our organisation can and should provide?' and 'What do I really want my organisation to accomplish so that I will be committed, aligned and proud of my association with the institution?'

The mission – be it written and widely distributed, or merely a set of widely held assumptions about the organization, has to be communicated to be useful. Its primary use, suggests Bennis, is to gain the attention of people at all levels of the organization, to focus their activities on a common, broad purpose. Out of the mission come objectives, which crystallize the generalization of the vision into tangible, realizable but still very broad goals. Strategy attempts to put those goals into a game plan. Tactics translate the game plan into specific objectives for individual elements of the organization.

In some of the companies we studied, such as Ogilvy & Mather, Johnson & Johnson, Black & Decker, 3M, IBM and JCB, the mission or credo has been carved in stone for a long time and is deeply ingrained in the company culture. In others it is a fairly recent development and attempts to crystallize elements of the culture that may always have been there but need the strength that comes from spelling them out. In the case of Cadbury Schweppes, Saatchi & Saatchi, ICL and Lansing, the style of the mission statement was very similar to that of long-established US companies. Just how natural to the genuinely British corporate mentality such statements of credo or mission really are, and how much they will become integrated into the company way of life, remains to be seen.

Among those companies that had long-established mission statements, three significant features emerged. The first was that the companies with the detailed missions tended to be of US parentage or were UK companies which operated in a noticeably American style, like JCB.

The second feature was the commitment to the corporate way of life represented by the credo. This was most clearly illustrated in the case of Johnson & Johnson, which demonstrated dramatically that much more than lip service was paid to its credo when it withdrew Tylenol from the shelves at a phenomenal cost. J&J spells out its credo in almost extreme detail. Its application is apparent in most areas of the business and it is quoted extensively by employees. Superficially it appears to be so comprehensive as to be virtually meaningless as a practical guide. In reality, however, it can be distilled down to the simple maxim of concern for its customers, its employees, its communities and its shareholders. There is no doubt that the management lives by this credo.

The third aspect is the fact that, although the business environment had often changed quite dramatically since the mission was established, there was no instance of the company appearing to be either old-fashioned or restricted in its operations – quite the contrary.

Some companies in the study had missions which were less well articulated or only came to light when probed for, but in each case the strategy was understood and influenced how the business operated. At Hi-Tec, for example, pragmatism appears to be the main influence. Similarly, Duracell's mission statement is very basic and simple.

Whether the direction of these companies is strictly defined or simply broad-brush, in all of them specific objectives are crystal clear.

Colin Marshall at British Airways knew exactly what he was going to achieve and how it would be done. He knew the company had to be able to respond quickly and sensitively to the changing needs of present and potential customers. He knew that extensive research was necessary to probe deeply into markets, customers, competitors and staff. The research was carried out and the conclusions were implemented effectively and quickly because he had already paved the way by convincing the employees of the seriousness of his mission.

Every weekday several BA directors, Marshall included, visit staff training courses and other events to talk with people about what the company is trying to do and why. Whenever he flies around the world Marshall leaves the plane at every opportunity, to talk to staff on duty.

All of this helps to change old attitudes. But the process was started by a series of actions which demonstrated that change really would happen. These ranged from a new livery and uniforms to firing the long-term advertising agency.

In TSB, Leslie Priestley clinically analysed what his competitors and potential competitors were doing, what his organization had available and what it could develop. Step by step he adapted his business to the fast-changing environment and the achievement of the objectives he set.

Cadbury found itself with problems which might or might not have been avoided. When they happened, however, Dominic Cadbury understood the dangers such a situation represented and that getting out of trouble fast was essential. The necessary action was taken quickly.

Bird's Eye left itself open to competitors and caught a bad cold, but it, too, learned its lesson, established very clear recovery objectives and appears to be achieving them. Smith's got itself into an even worse state, went back to basics, decided what it had to do and went full pelt after its new goals, having made sure that everyone understood the company's new direction.

Ever Ready suffered a different fate, but its vulnerability arose from the same indecisiveness and lack of knowing where it needed to go. Clark's temporarily let its objectives become clouded and suffered as a result.

In the case of ICL the situation was different. It was riding a strong wave when the tide turned. The rowing, which appeared fine going with the tide, became much harder with the ebb. ICL discovered that it had been the current, rather than the rowing, which had been controlling the ship, as many other companies in high-tech industries have also found to their cost. The channels and harbours have now been identified and the engine power necessary to get there has been installed.

Setting clear objectives appears so basic that we hesitated to consider it as a prime factor, but it became apparent that lack of such clarity was common to all the failure situations and increasingly it emerged as far from basic. Perhaps this realization explains the apparent oversimplicity of some mission statements. Business common sense is not as simple or as common as often assumed.

Certainly, in the consistently successful companies like IBM, 3M, Black & Decker, Rowntree Mackintosh, Beecham, JCB, BMW and Lansing, there is no doubt about where the organization is going and what it is going to achieve. In the recovery situations this clear mission is, if anything, more sharply defined, as exemplified in the new ICL objectives.

Two other elements were very apparent in the study. The companies not only set clear objectives, but they were ambitious – and in some cases very aggressively so in those objectives. Growth in line with inflation or industry average was not their style. Saatchi & Saatchi was to be the biggest in its field, would settle for nothing less and has achieved it. Cadbury, despite its problems, was going for number-two position in the world chocolate league. British Airways set its objectives as becoming the best and most successful airline in the world and it looks likely to achieve it. Hi-Tec has already achieved the number-two position in the UK sports footwear market; its goal is to move into the major international league. Jaguar is going to re-establish itself as the leading luxury car in the world's markets. JCB is taking on the best in the world and going for substantial growth.

Avis's Geoff Corbett doesn't bat an eyelid when he says that the corporate goal is 'to achieve our profit objectives by being the best rental and leasing company in the UK, via a creative and innovative approach to all customer requirements'. It was one of his predecessors, Robert Townsend, who wrote the remarkable management book *Up the Organisation*. As Townsend expressed it: 'If you can't do it excellently, don't do it at all. Because if it's not excellent it won't be profitable or fun and if you're not in business for fun or profit, what the hell are you doing here?'

The second element was the care these companies took to communicate their objectives throughout the organization. This was particularly clear in TSB where the new objectives represented a cultural change in the organization, with new attitudes and new methods of working.

To emphasize the bank's commitment to the new culture based on customer service it distributed a 'positioning statement' to each employee, detailing just what serving the customer meant and how the company intended to be perceived by those it serves. Leslie Priestley refers to this as the 'spirit' under which all medium- and long-term plans are prepared. Once the plans are drawn up they are communicated to all staff through regional conferences, branch meetings, video meetings and one-on-one meetings. The branch manager's annual objectives are prepared under a programme that stresses immediate action.

British Airways carried out massive communication exercises, aimed at making the new philosophy understood and deeply ingraining 'putting people first' attitudes. In Ogilvy & Mather creating the correct employee attitudes is a major senior management responsibility and is carried through with the same care and commitment as an important client presentation.

With Hertz, emphasis is placed on development from the bottom up of business plans within the established strategy. IBM carried out major communication programmes involving the chief executive and other senior management, to ensure that people know exactly what is expected from them. In his efforts to achieve fast and dramatic change in ICL, Peter Bonfield has committed massive human and financial resources to the reorientation of the whole organization and identification with the new corporate objectives. The company had already established itself as a pioneer in the regular use of video as a communications medium.

In Jaguar, John Egan took the communication of his objectives well beyond the Jaguar workforce. He went to suppliers and laid on the line what he was going to achieve, preferably with their involvement, but if necessary without it. The communications exercise was carried to distributors and customers, explaining what Jaguar was doing and the benefits which would derive from its successful implementation.

JCB and Lansing have highly developed communication programmes, both to ensure that objectives are understood and, equally importantly, to create enthusiasm and determination to achieve them. Avis has extensive communications programmes for staff which have achieved a very strong motivation and identification with the company.

At 3M, the new managing director, Ron Baukol, is carrying on the tradition of communicating market objectives directly to employees. In previous years, the managing director has issued a video, shown at every location. Baukol now aims to talk to everyone via a series of mass meetings around the country.

It is clear that far from being something to be taken for granted, the discipline of defining clear, ambitious, corporate objectives against the backcloth of the external and internal environment, of communicating them throughout the organization – and where appropriate to suppliers and customers – is an essential element in the armoury of successful companies. Equally clearly, it is all too often missing in those that fail.

Crunch highlights

Having a clearly defined mission, strategy and objectives is essential for concentrating minds and activities.

They have to be communicated, understood and accepted throughout the organization – top to bottom.

Objectives should be ambitious and demanding.

Understanding the market environment

When failures of established companies are analysed, certain features appear with disturbing regularity. These companies either lack the awareness that the market environment has changed, or they have failed to make the appropriate changes in operations and structure to fit themselves to the new situation. If they have responded to the new environment, they have not done so quickly enough.

Frequent and major change is now the rule in the majority of market environments. Take the following examples:

The slower rate of growth in many markets compared with the 1960s and 1970s.

The rapid rate of technological change.

The increasing importance of the service economy.

The shift in manufacturing as underdeveloped countries move into high-tech industries.

The saturation of markets, such as consumer electronics.

The social changes in attitudes to eating, drinking, smoking, equal opportunities and the environment.

The demographic changes, with their impact on products for children and old people.

The increase in corporate vulnerability of even major international groups like the Distillers Company.

The threats of terrorism and the impact of fear on travel which have had dramatic effects on airlines and hotels.

The impact of government decisions.

Anticipating and responding to the fast-changing competitive environment is fundamental to the success of the companies in the study, and losing this deftness of touch was the basic reason for the troubles some of them had experienced. British Caledonian and British Airways, in common with other airlines heavily involved in the North Atlantic routes, faced a dramatic fall in their traffic and had to respond. Both did so successfully. Other industries have been less successful. While the tobacco companies have accepted the inevitable decline in cigarette consumption in developed countries and have taken steps to adapt, many of them have encountered severe setbacks in their attempts to diversify. Only recently have they begun to show the skill at adapting to change which they need to be successful in their new market ventures. The packaging business is even further adrift. It has yet to grasp the nettle of changes in consumer attitudes, in self-service retailing and in manufacturing technology. Though technology developments in plastics have altered the whole market environment for glass and cans, many packaging firms show a continuing reluctance to accept that the market has changed. Their failure to react to or pre-empt change is causing an increasingly painful decline in many cases, leaving them vulnerable to more ruthless predators who will take the much more drastic action that is now essential.

Two other factors are also fundamental in these market environment considerations. The first is that the company must determine the full range of influences impacting on its markets. The second is that having a mass of data is not by itself the answer, if understanding does not accompany it. The desk drawers of executives of unsuccessful companies are often stacked high with half-read, unactioned research reports.

Over recent years there has been a change in attitude and practice in many of the fast-moving consumer goods companies which had traditionally operated on a mechanistic research-to-death approach. Little if anything was decided or accepted unless detailed research was provided to support it. In a growth-market environment, the reason for success was often credited to research when in fact many other hunch products were often equally successful, because the market was buoyant. With lower growth and much greater competition, attitudes have changed as it became clear that research could not guarantee success, and that often the time necessary to carry out the exhaustive probing could mean the opportunity was lost as some competitor moved in or the environment changed yet again. Effective monitoring of the environment is real time. It calls for decisions on what is happening now and what can be predicted for the mid-term future. Research is balanced with more subjective know-how to take action, rather than to stimulate discussion.

The need now is for a much more careful analysis of what really influences a particular market and greater emphasis on understanding, interpretation and judgement. This changed thinking is very apparent in most of the companies in the study and is in tune with what we now know about the way successful executives make decisions. They do not, as commonly supposed, examine problems and opportunities in immense detail and with laborious logic before deciding what to do. Effective decisions are taken on a partially intuitive basis, drawing upon a number of key pieces of information. Further research is used not to make or unmake the decision but to clarify the tactical detail.

Understanding of the customer at top management level is not enough, however. That understanding has to be communicated to all levels and particularly to the product development functions. This was emphasized recently by Project Sappho, a survey of successful and unsuccessful innovation by British companies in two sectors – chemical processing and scientific instruments. One factor that stood out with great clarity was that the successful innovators understood their users' needs better than unsuccessful innovators. Seems obvious? So it is; yet many, perhaps the majority of innovations, fail precisely because the company has failed to see its product or service from the user's point of view. Rowntree Mackintosh considered it was in the pleasure, happiness and emotional satisfaction business and that products and advertising should have this approach. This was very apparent in the whole approach to Yorkie, as it probed what people looked for in a bar of chocolate and found that their expectations were not being fully satisfied by existing products, which had been made smaller and flatter for cost reasons. Carefully planned and analysed research indicated that consumers wanted the emotional satisfaction of a real bite of chocolate. It also found they had other image perceptions, which were very influential and were not being fully satisfied by existing competitive products. A further example . . . Black Magic chocolates satisfy another emotional need and have provided romantic satisfaction for over fifty years and will probably continue to do so.

TSB has analysed its markets and the influences on them in considerable detail. It has identified what was important to its customers in general and in specific segments. The outcome has been a culture change throughout the organization to make it clear to customers that they matter above all. TSB also identified the increasingly important segment of elderly customers and it custom-built the products to meet the needs of that market.

The care TSB took to gain a thorough understanding of what interested and motivated young people in the fifteen to nineteen age bracket convinced it that it should not offer 'give-aways' as the competition did. It discovered that people of that age valued service rather than gimmicks and adjusted its pitch accordingly, to seize a significant share of the market. Nearly one-third of all school leavers who opened a cheque account in 1985 did so with the TSB. Sensitivity to the things that caused most annoyance to bank customers convinced TSB that it should follow the Midland to introduce free banking. The other three big banks took a year to do the same. Meanwhile, the TSB saw its customers' cheque account balances grow by 18%.

In the airline business the planes are essentially identical, costs are similar and influencing customers' choice of airline depended on understanding what other factors mattered to them. British Airways carried out in-depth research to identify what these factors were, against an international political and economic environment which was constantly changing. It identified both what customers in general needed to ease the general white-knuckles problem, and what was needed to satisfy specific segment needs. Recognizing that quality of service is what counts in the long term, BA conducts monthly customer relations analyses, looking not only for what might be going wrong, but where there might be an opportunity to steal a march on the competition. These reports go to top management, where Marshall personally signs the replies to all letters written to him. Surveys by travel magazines are scrutinized in detail, particularly when some aspect of BA's service attracts adverse comment. One survey revealed, for example, that passengers often thought the still wines were awful by comparison with those served by other airlines. Investigation showed that the problem was concentrated on certain routes, where wine in screw-top bottles could be stored too long. The solution was to change the distribution and supply arrangements to make sure that flights from, say Australia, were locally sourced to prevent deterioration with age. British Caledonian research was concentrated on more limited market areas. Although the assessment was similar to BA's, it chose a different emphasis in terms of satisfying customer needs and majored on the care and professionalism of the Caledonian Girls.

Beecham's attitude to its markets has undergone change from one of intensive research and testing to much greater judgement and risk taking. It has read the changing environment and recognized that building a new brand is excessively expensive when there are available in many markets well-known but underdeveloped brands which could respond strongly to the Beecham treatment. Its attitude to market research is very pragmatic. Beecham uses research to identify changing life styles and fashions, to support change and innovation within brands, not to accumulate market data for the sake of it.

Hi-Tec Sports has an even more pragmatic approach. It uses little formal market research, but keeps very close to what is said and written by authorities in its markets and what its competitors do. Clark's carries out extensive research on social, fashion, life-style and technological changes; and this orientation to knowing what is happening in its markets was the main reason for moving into retailing in the 1930s.

In the luxury car market, where any particular feature of motoring could be provided quite adequately by cheaper alternatives, providing perceived benefits is critically important. So is the need for a deep understanding of what influences customers' choice. For Jaguar this understanding was especially critical and it invested enormous effort into researching its market. That research paid off in numerous ways, not least in the launch of its much-heralded new vehicle, the XJ40. Recognizing that so much of customer attitudes was based on expectations, the company was able to turn the continuing delays in launching the new car from a liability to an asset. The aura of mystery created by subtle hints over a period of two years and more gave the company a level of press comment and speculation previously achieved only by IBM with the launch of its personal computer. John Egan and his marketing team deliberately made the car and its launch date into a game, telling shareholders at the annual general meeting that the car would be launched 'later this year ... or next'. Although this approach inevitably led to a downturn in sales of the old model, the XJ6, in the months leading up to the launch, the dealers expressed themselves as more than happy, because of the continued and carefully fuelled speculation. BMW, on the other hand, has a much wider range of vehicles and so could use a much less specific pitch and an appeal based on an image of the discriminating, individualistic driver. Making this strategy work requires both careful understanding of emotional influences and constant attention to reinforcing them.

It is not by accident that Black & Decker has positioned itself in the vanguard of the DIY and general leisure markets. It was one of the first companies to accept that successful innovation and introduction of new products required a rounded understanding of what was happening economically, socially and demographically in the developed countries, and to identify how the changing environment could be exploited. Black & Decker analyses the changing life style, the activities which this will stimulate (whether out of desire or necessity), the characteristics of the people involved and their shopping habits. Exploiting this situation requires a progression of clearly identified new products, which Black & Decker aims to supply from its own or outside resources.

In some ways, 3M could be accused of creating products and then looking for market needs which they will satisfy, and to some extent this is true. However, its approach is far from the traditional 'sell what is being produced' mentality. It accepts that successful product innovation requires creative freedom, but within a clearly defined strategy, which channels the thinking behind innovation along established lines or within parameters defined to a large extent by market requirements. 3M accepts that more and more business will come from fewer and fewer customers and recognizes that it is essential to know in depth what is happening within those customer companies. Its approach is an acknowledgement that in a constantly changing environment, influenced by customers, governments, retailers and different life styles, it is important to have a regular and plentiful supply of new products on the shelf, which can be introduced as necessary. With such a heavy investment in technological innovation it is essential that this is carried out in an environment of market-place understanding and two-way traffic.

The depth of understanding of a market can significantly affect the speed with which a company can react to a competitive threat. 3M's diagnostic imaging group, which produces a high-resolution film for X-ray machines, found itself the victim of National Health Service cuts. Because its product Trimax used rare earths in its composition, it cost 10% more than competitive products and cost-conscious central supply units in the NHS were buying the cheaper alternatives.

The options for 3M were to discount the price or to demonstrate that Trimax was cheaper in operation. So 3M carried out extensive tests in hospitals to determine the overall costs of using its product, versus the costs of using the competition's products. It then convinced radiographers that the superior product added 20% to the life of the expensive radiation tubes, reduced power consumption and capital costs of construction, and resulted in both fewer operator errors and less wastage. With the resulting pressure from the hospital users – the end-customers – 3M restored and stabilized its market.

Ever Ready has learned from its earlier lack of concern for what was happening in its markets. As often happens, it has tended to over-research and provide data more as a public relations feature than for decision-making. However, within the mass of data, it does have an understanding of what is likely to affect its markets and is making decisions which pay full regard to the real situation.

With the rate of change in information technology (both technological development and growth) there is a comparison to be drawn with the original industrial revolution. Then, as now, numerous companies grew fast and profitably on new developments, which arose out of basic technological boffinry rather than market understanding. As the situation has changed, many entrepreneurial companies have paid the price of not adequately understanding their market situation.

IBM has seen such companies come and go while it stayed consistently successful and its message has continued to be: 'Remember, the customer pays your salary.' IBM ensures that it maintains its market position and customer influence by understanding fully what changes are taking place both internationally, in national markets and in specific market segments. This information is considered critically important for the continuation of IBM's competitive edge and for making it possible to exploit new opportunities.

Understanding its competitive environment is an integral part of ICL's new philosophy, as is knowing precisely where it is going and the markets on which it will concentrate its activities. Extensive research into its market-place, leading to product and organizational development, is at the core of ICL's strategic thinking.

Perhaps the most surprising was the extent of JCB's awareness and understanding in great depth of the influences, threats and opportunities in its international markets. Not only did it analyse this information, but its management system ensured that the conclusions were communicated to engineering design and finance areas which, with marketing, drew conclusions on how JCB could translate information into a competitive edge.

Lansing also puts great stress on understanding its markets. Says joint managing director Derek Larkins: 'We achieve this by continuously investigating existing materials-handling applications in numerous environments, in worldwide markets. We discuss our ideas with current and future customers and, as necessary, subject to confidentiality, with suppliers and with professional bodies both technical and commercial. Equally important, we listen to advice given by those of our employees who have a detailed knowledge of what they consider influences the environment and markets in which we operate.'

That the companies we examined should have this deep understanding of their market environment came as no surprise. Quite the contrary. However, from other studies over the last two years, it would appear that many companies do not use formal marketing research and are unaware of how their markets are changing. The lack of such basic awareness in operating a business is difficult to comprehend, but on a more positive note it points to the gains which could be achieved if these companies were competitive with their eyes open rather than closed.

Crunch highlights

The market environment is constantly changing.

Companies must comprehend the *full* range and extent of influences impacting their markets.

Market and competition data is for understanding and assisting in decision-making – not for storing.

Assessing the assets

A clear understanding of the market and the forces operating within it is an essential prerequisite for making a realistic assessment of the assets of the company, its strengths and weaknesses, and how they could be used to maximum advantage. Many companies tend to overestimate the strengths and underestimate the weaknesses, and the company assessment both of the overall situation and of what elements are important often differs from that of its customers.

This was exemplified in the packaging industry in the late 1960s, when competition became intense. Manufacturers of packaging considered that what their customers wanted from their sales team was specialist expert knowledge of the particular packaging product. So they structured the marketing and technical back-up to provide exactly that. This attitude resulted from the traditional belief that packaging companies were in the business of selling the products they produced. Research into the attitudes and needs of the purchaser of packaging materials indicated precisely the opposite. They took for granted that the salesman would have specialist knowledge of his product, and the influencing factor in selecting a packaging supplier was how much the company and its salesmen knew about the conditions and problems in the *buyer's* markets and, even more importantly, how they could help the buyer to improve his market performance.

Arising out of this realization came the fundamental restructuring of the packaging industry, with a market orientation replacing the previous product orientation. At the same time the sales, marketing, technical development and service back-up were structured to understand and support a group of customer markets with common features and needs. This structure acknowledged the fact that although, for example, the whisky, dairy, toiletries and pharmaceutical industries all used glass containers, their needs in terms of product presentation, distribution, competition and customer appeal were quite different. The packaging company needed to understand that and tailor its approach accordingly.

Until a company really understands what makes its customers tick, it is difficult to make a realistic assessment of its own strengths and weaknesses. It is important to understand that what is a strength at one time can become a weakness in a changed market environment.

Bird's Eye had the Unilever refrigerated distribution system as its major strength in the early period of frozen foods and appeared to think that advantage would remain indefinitely. When frozen-food distributors opened up, Bird's Eye competitors did not have the penalty of their own structure to support and could exploit the new situation much more effectively.

Smith's Crisps had the strength of its distributed manufacturing units. While these were costly, they met the needs of a short-life product. When new packaging extended the shelf life, its competitors, who did not have Smith's spread of factories, were able to achieve an economic edge by installing larger production units.

Many British companies consider their brand name and the fact that they are British as their major assets in the market. Yet whole industries which held the same view have disappeared in the face of virtually unknown, foreign competitors who had taken the trouble to understand the changing needs of customers and satisfy those needs with a good-quality, well-priced product.

Jaguar saw its superb brand strength disappearing fast in the face of quality complaints and poor service, and was under no illusions about what would happen if it did not act fast to correct the weaknesses and re-establish the Jaguar reputation for quality, performance and style. Having now done that, it is fully aware that it has much to do to improve other aspects: fuel economy, instrumentation and appearance have all to be advanced.

By contrast, British Caledonian, as the David competing with international airline Goliaths, has never taken anything for granted in its fight to survive against national airlines. It constantly appraises its strengths and weaknesses against the market needs, and concentrates on developing its unique Caledonian Girl asset in a business where care and reassurance are paramount.

British Airways does no less. Its new strategy was based on a thorough appreciation of the strength of its operations (it was seen as exceptionally safe, with the best-trained aircrew in the world) and of the weakness of its customer service. The remedy lay in large part in restoring the faith of the cabin staff in the company and in their own managers, who had by and large become remote from the day-to-day problems of the staff. 'It was no good their telling a steward with a problem: "I know, I used to do it twenty years ago",' comments a BA manager. The solution was to put the managers back into the air, working alongside the cabin crew they supervise, where they could obtain up-to-date, first-hand experience of customer service problems.

In assessing its strengths and weaknesses, Avis determined that it could not compete effectively on price. Instead, it looked hard at the needs of its primary customers, business travellers, and built upon its strengths in speed and efficiency of service.

A major Beecham strength was the ability to extract the maximum benefit out of brands through segmentation and to create perceived benefits to match the customer needs it identified in the market. Exploiting these skills became a major part of its corporate expansion strategy and this, in turn, strengthened the development of such talents in its management in a constantly reinforcing cycle. Beecham has a track record of acquiring companies with good but declining brands relatively cheaply. Its management strengths have permitted it to implement rapid brand-development and stretching strategies, and thus to achieve a return on investment over a very short period.

The more honestly a company assesses its assets internally and in the market-place, the more straightforward it will find its decisions on alternative market-strategies. Cadbury-Schweppes carried out such an exercise and came to two key conclusions: that its major assets were the Cadbury and Schweppes brands; and that its future strength lay in the development of these two international brands in confectionery and drinks, rather than in spreading its resources more thinly across other food and hygiene products. As a result, it divested itself of the peripheral activities and concentrated its resources on its mainstream activities.

Clark's saw its strengths as its understanding and involvement in the footwear business from manufacture through to retailing. It considered that if it could not be successful in the business it knew deeply, then it was unlikely to be so in a different business. Sticking to its last and doing it well became the prime driving force. With Hi-Tec, the situation was quite different. It considered its marketing dynamism and procurement skills were its key assets and the natural development was to use these to bring in new associated products. In this way it broadened its base and achieved dramatic growth.

The assets of Black & Decker are under constant assessment as it reviews itself against its changing business environment. With its emphasis on new-product development and innovation it cannot risk missing out on opportunities, and it sees its primary strengths as the ability to read the market better and exploit it faster and more effectively than competitors. Since it is in the business of making life easier for consumers in a fast-moving market strongly influenced by technology and social change, it is very quickly aware of any shortcomings in its assumed assets.

3M has a similar emphasis on innovational activity and new-product development, but sees its strength in an ability to identify '3M's unfair advantage'. It does not necessarily aim to be first in a market but to have a competitive edge. While Black & Decker tends to develop a product to meet an identified market need, 3M tends to work in the opposite direction. Its company environment filters new developments into well-researched and understood market areas where they can be linked to existing latent or in-cipient needs. To generate this wider catchment and exploitation of new developments, 3M spends more than 6% of its turnover on research.

In the information technology sector, the speed of change means that today's strength is tomorrow's weakness, and the industry is awash with the wrecks of companies built on the strength of a single bright innovation. In such an environment of shooting stars, IBM has managed its business effectively and profitably, and has grown consistently as competitors came and went. Its strength is quite simply that it is a very well-managed, strongly market-oriented organization. It adapts effectively to the changing market environment in structure, attitudes and operations because the whole organization understands and accepts the implications of the information-technology business. Its prime strength is its ability to be flexible and match its total approach to the needs of the market, which it appraises on a continuous basis.

ICL developed its strengths to match the environment of the 1970s, but they were found wanting in the recession of the early 1980s. The task of the present management has been to reorient the business to the new competitive environment while developing the strengths appropriate to the rest of the decade and beyond.

The strengths of JCB and Lansing are remarkably similar. JCB concentrates on specific activities, does not allow itself to be sidetracked, and understands in detail what it needs to do to satisfy customers better than its competitors do. Lansing concentrates on business fundamentals, aims to combine the flexibility of a small company with the stability of a large organization and is dedicated to being better than its competitors in meeting its customers' needs through its 'total-involvement' approach.

Lansing is also helped by what it calls its 'open style of management' – the encouragement of frank discussion of business issues, where people do not feel they have to hide real or potential problems. Says Derek Larkins: 'We believe that any other style of management is not likely to give the right breadth of consideration on positive and negative situations. We strongly believe in converting problems to opportunities. Today's complaint should be tomorrow's sale.

'There should be no shirking from face-to-face discussion between management and employees, and management and unions. But no amount of discussions should become an excuse for not getting things done. Taking no action is sometimes the right solution, but such a course should be explained to those involved in the events leading up to such a decision.'

Both companies have been consistently successful in international markets. Once again their key strength is the commitment and flexibility in meeting the needs of a changing, highly competitive market environment.

One common link through all the companies is that they have honestly assessed their positive and negative assets. As a result of that knowledge they have developed both their strengths and their ability to win in the current market-place.

Also important is the frequency with which companies make this kind of analysis. At TSB it is a formal annual process, with informal reviews as necessary. Recognizing its relative weakness in the commercial finance sector it has taken decisive action, including revamping its branch network to concentrate commercial business in 300 key branches, recruiting experienced commercial lending staff, particularly from the large clearing banks, and investing heavily in training to develop the necessary skills. Many units of Saatchi carry out six-monthly examinations of their strengths and weaknesses. Other companies in the study review their strengths and weaknesses almost continuously, because they recognize how rapidly a competitive stronghold can be undermined by events.

We observed at the beginning of this section that a realistic assessment of strengths and weaknesses depended on a real understanding of the company's markets. There is, however, one further essential ingredient – courage. It takes a special kind of leadership, an innate, unselfconscious confidence to be able to step back from the company one heads and assess it objectively. It takes even greater courage to listen to honest criticism by other people, inside or outside. The chief executive who has sufficient confidence in his own ability and that of his management team to *invite*, welcome and endorse such objective assessment is well on the way to market success, if not already there.

Crunch highlights

Only when a company understands its markets can it assess its positive and negative assets.

With a constantly changing market environment, strengths can become weaknesses and vice versa.

The assessment of assets has to be honest and objective.

Market segmentation

One of the most striking features of the companies studied was their understanding of why market segmentation was necessary in markets undergoing increasing complexity and rapidity of change. Other research has shown a surprising lack of segmentation by British companies in general. It seems that many companies base their approach on the belief that markets are not really different and that, in any case, their products have a universal appeal. It is doubtful if that were ever completely true. Certainly, as purchasers become more sophisticated, the company that identifies particular needs and produces a product to satisfy them will normally be more successful than the company that produces only a general-purpose alternative. The logic is so basic that it is a mystery why so many companies continue to ignore it.

All the companies in the study took it for granted that they must segment markets. The difference in their approaches lay mainly in the degree of refinement they applied. It was also apparent that these companies understood the factors which could erode the effectiveness of segmentation, but often create further segmentation opportunities such as:

Technological change.
Social trends.
Government legislation.
Market saturation.
Competitors' segmentation.
Cost changes.
Fashion and style fads.

They also understood the importance of fast exploitation and the timing of a move to another segment.

To segment a market properly you must understand it thoroughly. Raw market-research data will not normally provide that understanding. If it does, then the lack of refinement will make it easy for competitors to follow.

Segmentation is fundamental to successful marketing strategies. Until competitors copy or segment your segmentation, you have a competitive edge, even if you serve the segment with a standard product or service. If the product is specific to the segment then your competitive advantage is multiplied.

The Strategic Planning Institute of Cambridge, Massachusetts holds data on hundreds of companies across the world in its PIMS (Profit Impact of Market Strategy) project. PIMS analyses indicate incontrovertibly that, over the long haul, the companies with the highest returns are those that pick viable niches, achieve a leadership position within them and provide a high value-added product or service.

Beecham has a particular talent for identifying market segments and often takes it to a niche level. It takes an established product such as Ribena and identifies niches with different needs. It then fulfils those needs with precisely targeted variations of a different packaging (cartons, cans, bottles, large or small); different versions of the product: ready-to-drink, sparkling, concentrated, mixed, or flavour (for babies, teenagers, mothers, old people). The growth in outdoor sporting activities prompted the pitching of Lucozade as a healthy sportsman's drink, although it had traditionally been almost exclusively associated with invalids. By understanding the variations of its markets and by being imaginative, Beecham has created unique opportunities for high-margin niche products. It has done so with remarkable regularity, not only in drinks but across the whole range of its products.

Abbey National understood the difficulties home buyers meet in moving fast on a purchase and produced the mortgage certificate to meet that specific need. It identified the building society cash culture as one of the few disadvantages its customers faced compared with banks, and it produced the simple cheque account. Both of these things could have been made available by other societies, but Abbey National's research and understanding of its customers provided the raw material for identifying segment opportunities. Abbey has recently restructured its organization to focus even more closely on niche markets. It now has four core businesses, all of which are regarded as strategic business units – transactions (covering traditional current-account needs); thrift (covering longer-term savings); protection (covering insurance and similar services); and lending (covering credit services). Each of these businesses is expected to develop its own range of sub-niches.

TSB analysed its customer profile and the special features of each group of customers, and saw the potential for creating tailor-made products for the very distinct and special needs of the elderly segment of its market. It has a project team specifically charged with identifying niche markets and products to fill them. This team is building upon a track record that includes a number of spectacular successes, among them the bank's Speedsend service to enable solicitors to settle transactions more swiftly and easily. Within three years of start-up this service was handling some 140,000 transactions annually. Another niche market was discovered in the overdraft market, where TSB business customers can now have a combined cheque, interest-bearing account and overdraft facilities negotiated at the outset. The bank attracted 10,000 new business accounts with this service during 1985.

British Caledonian knew it could not compete across the board against the major airlines, nor could it hope to win on hardware. It identified the special features of the business traveller segment and pieced together a package which would make the airline distinctive and appealing to that type of passenger.

BA, as one of the largest airlines in the world, covers most major market segments. But it also makes extensive use of niche strategies within each of those segments. The number of flights to, say Aberdeen, is maintained by cultivating North American oilmen en route to the United States. Similarly, BA has carved itself a major chunk of the business from the Persian Gulf and India to the United States, by making the flights (including a stopover in London) as convenient as possible, with cabin crew who speak Urdu, Arabic and Pakistani. The company admits, however, that it has learnt a lesson or two in this kind of business from the Dutch airline, KLM, which has taken Schipol from a minor European backwater to a major international travel nexus.

Hertz, which was generally seen as providing all things for all people in the car-hire business, discovered the disadvantage of such a commodity approach and moved to rifle-shot market segmentation with its specially tailored Business Class and American vacation visitor packages. The features of each package were developed out of deep research into the life style and special needs of the two customer segments.

Avis, too, identified the American visitor as a key market segment. Its research into customer needs generated the Personally Yours programme, which provides the US visitor with computer-generated individual itineraries. The programme is backed up by a touring guide aimed specifically at this segment.

Bird's Eye, in the early days, saw frozen foods as a single market and treated it as almost a commodity operation, in which it had virtually a monopolistic control through its distribution system. Despite the wisdom of hindsight, such an attitude was understandable, if still surprising, for a company in the market-aware Unilever group. The impact of changing life styles, self-service retail power and aggressive competitors forced Bird's Eye to investigate and understand its market better, and in the clarification exercise it recognized that it was certainly in frozen-food distribution, but in a wide range of different food product markets. To maintain its position Bird's Eye had no choice but to search out market segments and niches where its considerable strengths could give it an advantage. Creative innovation replaced the previous distribution dominance and the company is pulling back its market share through well thought-through, soundly based marketing.

Smith's carried out a similar heart-searching exercise, went back to marketing fundamentals and through very disciplined research identified where its opportunities lay in the non-crisp snack market, particularly with its specialist manufacturing strength in extruded foods.

Rowntree was faced with the tremendously strong Cadbury name in chocolate. Early on, it determined that its main weapons had to be imaginative market segmentation, product innovation and strong branding. Out of this thinking came developments such as Black Magic, Aero, Smarties and Yorkie, aimed at very specific market segments and promoted with a strong emotional content to appeal to the particular customer groups. It is interesting that Cadbury is now moving in a similar direction.

The Schweppes half of the organization produced a model of creative market segmentation in the late 1960s. At that time it dominated the mixer drink market which had been essentially a bar or wine-shop business. With the growth of self-service supermarkets it found itself under pressure from competitors packaging mixers in cans, which were the only packaging supermarkets would accept. The supermarkets insisted they were not prepared to handle the deposit complications of returnable bottles and pointed out that cans withstood rough handling better. Schweppes found that mixers were increasingly becoming a commodity business. In an effort to protect its market share and its brand, it carried out extensive research into consumer perceptions and preferences in mixer drinks, into how they were used and into the attitudes of consumers and retailers towards different packages.

It discovered that one of its packaging suppliers had carried out an almost parallel exercise. Both studies arrived at the same conclusion – that if a special glass container could be developed to match the desirable features of the can, the market segment using mixers would much prefer the convenience and perceived purity of glass. This would enable Schweppes to regain its unique identity. The outcome was the quarter-litre, non-returnable, toughened, light-weight bottle, which is still the dominant package in the mixer business. It not only enabled Schweppes to regain its brand dominance but also provided the massive volume increase the glass-container industry needed – the double benefit of creative market segmentation and product innovation.

Johnson & Johnson's prime market segment is baby care and it has been so constantly successful that its brand name has become almost generic. Mothercare was another company which researched the baby market in depth and found it serviced by a variety of retail outlets: prams from bicycle shops, clothes from chain stores, toys from department stores, feeding utensils from chemists. Mothercare brought them all together and provided a single shop where parents could buy all their special requirements for the new baby and the infant. Competition overtook Mothercare but Johnson & Johnson handled a potentially similar situation more successfully, and the company is now setting its sights at the forty-plus women's segment.

Clark's is another company that identified the children's segment as a major opportunity. Like Johnson & Johnson, it has come to dominate its chosen niche by imaginative research and by understanding what it has to do to meet the special needs.

The three special talents of Black & Decker are identifying interesting market segments in the making-life-easier business, understanding what is important to people in those segments and having the resources internally and externally to develop appropriate products. Its consistent success in these activities arises from disciplined and carefully planned analysis of what is happening in its existing and potential markets, and the ability to link product to market opportunity better and faster than competitors do.

The 'Post it' notes developed by 3M illustrate the other side of the coin, the product looking for its market. The needs were there, but they needed to be exposed and cultivated, and they were so wide-ranging that explosive growth was likely as awareness spread. 3M's innovative approach was to send sample packs to thousands of managing directors and their secretaries, and ask them how they used 'Post it' notes.

Supasnaps, a 3M division selling film developing and processing through a national chain of 350 shops, found itself competing more and more on price. By intelligent segmentation it focused its promotional activities upon those photographers who wanted higher quality from their prints. Its 'Custom 35' service offers more rigorous checking of print production and an automatic reprocessing of any print where the inspector feels that more could be got out of the negative. A significant proportion of its customers have now converted to this higher priced, more profitable service.

Ever Ready, after a history of near-neglect of its market, found itself at the point when decisions on future development could no longer be delayed and the obvious but expensive route was to simply follow Duracell along the alkaline battery route. The challenge was to minimize the financial cost and if possible turn the market situation to Ever Ready's advantage. Research and imaginative reading of the market achieved exactly that, with the introduction of the zinc chloride battery. This product used Ever Ready's existing zinc production capability and was also probably the best all-round value for money. It enabled Ever Ready to play two hands and manage its zinc carbon development in a much more controlled way, while taking the battle to the competition with the new product.

Marketing segmentation is central to IBM's strategy. It researches and analyses continuously with the basic objective of gaining a competitive edge in existing or new markets. It makes organizational changes and develops new products to match the identified needs of clearly defined market segments. The flexibility to adapt to the new demands is critical to IBM's success.

Market segmentation is a core feature of all the companies in the study, and particularly of consistently successful ones. By contrast, it often happens that companies abandon segmentation as their markets mature or decline. There is an apparent logic to so doing – after all, surely the only way to maintain economies of scale in such circumstances is to progressively standardize? The problem is that this all too frequently removes the product differential that made particular customer groups choose that product as opposed to its competitors. A better strategy may be to focus more closely on specific customer groups, gaining good margins from high value added, rather than high volume.

The whole point about a niche is that it is often small and easily defended. It is also different from the rest of the broad market. So it is that, even in the most mature markets, there are usually niche segments that are growing rapidly and where higher margins are readily available. In almost all cases, those niches had to be created.

In the end it all boils down to how creatively a company looks at its market-place and how well it understands it; how accurately and closely a company defines the segment for a particular product offering; and how it responds to the opportunities it perceives there.

Imaginative segmentation can identify a host of viable new opportunities in an apparently mature market. Unimaginative segmentation simply tends to average out critical differences between groups of customers. By simply assuming that certain types of people have the same basic needs which can be met by the same basic product, companies ignore market segmentation to meet the demands from the production floor and often gain efficiency at the expense of effectiveness.

Segmentation is so fundamental and so in keeping with the natural variety of customer differences, that to fail to operate a business on such a basis is to deny the basic reality of customer choice.

Crunch highlights

Segmentation is fundamental to successful marketing strategies.
Markets are becoming increasingly complex and subject to change. (Niches can open and close rapidly.)
Segmentation needs to be meaningful and imaginative.

Knowing the competition

Knowing competitors is the other side of the market coin from knowing the customers. It is equally critical in the ultimate goal of establishing a differential advantage for the company's product or service. If there has been a reluctance in some companies to pay full regard to customers' needs, there has been just as little attention paid to competitors and their activities. An examination of most companies' business plans (or more specifically, their marketing plans), would reveal very little knowledge or analysis of competitors' current activity or how competitors are likely to respond to the company's strategy.

Just as many executives find that direct customer selling is stressful, they also shy away from the conflict aspect of handling competitors. This unease in a competitive environment appears to be deeply entrenched in some national cultures, and particularly in the UK. Playing the game still too often seems to be considered as important if not more important than winning. Business and especially the customer/competitor environment is all about winning, and it is one in which many executives feel uncomfortable.

The US culture is quite the opposite. Winners are acclaimed and losers are forgotten. In Japan, the penalty for loss of face does not allow besting by a competitor to be accepted as anything other than temporary.

Attitudes in the UK began to change as the comfortable industrial superiority and protected market environment disappeared with the Second World War and British companies had to face increasingly severe international competition. Education and social changes, and the greater attraction of industrial and commercial careers, are developing an acceptance that competitive attitudes and commitment are necessary for success in a vastly changed environment. But our competitors are already way ahead.

As awareness of the impact of competition grew, so also did the interest in what the competition was doing. The greater the competition, the more necessary and detailed such understanding became.

Clearly, the type of business influences the kind of intelligence needed about the competition: the emphasis in a consumer goods or services company will differ from that in an industrial company. This difference was very apparent in the companies studied.

In the industrial category, JCB had literally taken apart its international competitors' products. It dissected and examined their physical products in detail. JCB also probed the manufacturing operations, the types of machine tools used, their speeds, manning levels, labour costs, quality control and testing procedures, and raw-material and energy prices. It built up a profile of all its main competitors' operations and performance ratios against which it compared itself. In this way, the company knew the extent to which competitors could play the price game, what their strengths and weaknesses were and how JCB could exploit the advantages it had.

This approach is very reminiscent of many US companies, which take competitor comparisons to quite remarkable lengths, particularly in commodity type products. This same approach became much more common in Europe during the 1979–84 recession, when excess supply in many industries brought severe price competition and when labour, raw material and energy costs could make or break a company. Similarly, different government practices on fuel tax and basic raw-material prices, or policies on pay restraint, could have a major impact on the competitive position in international markets of a nation's industries.

Lansing has a similarly analytical approach to its competitors. Like JCB, while it accepts the need to be cost competitive, it has focused very strongly on added value to avoid price comparisons. To be successful in this kind of approach requires a deep understanding of what competitors are doing and where opportunities exist for developing added-value features.

Most airlines in the Western world have to submit so much data on their activities to regulatory authorities that it is relatively easy to analyse almost every aspect of their operations. Most also send staff to take and report back on competitors' flights. BA has increased its efforts in this area substantially under the current management, having now created a market-place comparison department reporting directly to the chief executive. This department has responsibility for producing a detailed analysis of a different major competitor each month.

In most markets the direct competitors are normally readily apparent. Less apparent but often a greater threat are indirect competitors. Cadbury's and Rowntree's presentation boxes of chocolates were once the main personal gifts in social situations. Now they have been largely replaced by wine, flowers and plants.

In the leisure business both direct and indirect competition abounds. Sport, entertainment, DIY and gardening all compete for customer spending. Competition in the clothes market for young people is severe, but the alternative to a shirt from one store is not only a different shirt from another store, but also a record or tape or a piece of gadgetry for a motorbike.

The essence of identifying competitors is identifying the real business the company is in, and it is often much wider than first appears, as Levitt pointed out very clearly in his *Marketing Myopia*.

In the soft-drinks business, packaging suppliers were so involved with fighting between glass, cans and plastic that they almost overlooked the increasing switch to pump dispensing, particularly in bars.

The level of market saturation also has a major influence on indirect competition. This was very apparent in the TV market when virtually every home had one set. The competitive considerations involved in a replacement or second set were very different from those which applied on the first purchase. The first was an essential, the second was an added convenience. The age of prospective purchasers can also have a considerable effect on what the competing pressures will be, as can the socio-economic status. To the young, home-building family the alternative to a new carpet could be a fridge; to an elderly couple it could be a second holiday.

Identifying the likely competition requires a real understanding of what matters to the prospective purchaser and what his or her attitudes and perceptions are. This in turn requires an awareness of life style and of social, environmental and political change.

As self-service retailing developed and emphasis was concentrated on shelf space, the competitor to a particular product could be an apparently unrelated item that gave a better return for the space it used. This was, and still is, particularly noticeable at or near the checkout area. The growth in own-label products brought another new element to competition, and changed significantly the market strategy of manufacturers whose brand was competing with that of a major customer. In many consumer products this has developed to the stage where the major competition comes not from other manufacturers but from customers' own brands, and even major brand companies are finding the going very tough.

The response of most companies has been to strengthen their branding. However, in some cases, such as Marks & Spencer, Sainsbury or Boots, the retailer brand is also nationally accepted. So this strategy, while essential, may still be only partially effective in restraining competition.

In the information-technology business the rate of change and the scope for fast entrepreneurial growth produced new competitors in abundance. Many – indeed most – of them fell by the wayside. In such a situation, IBM placed emphasis on anticipating what competitors were likely to do rather than on responding when it had happened. In this way it was able either to beat them to the punch or effectively blunt their moves. Bird's Eye's awakening to competition in frozen foods exemplifies the need for constant vigilance even, and probably especially, when you hold the dominant share in the market. Other competitive threats are developing as interest increases in healthier eating and more natural food, but this time Bird's Eye is probably ultra sensitive to any such danger. It could, of course, over-react and therein lies a danger for companies newly awakened to competitive marketing.

Ever Ready was so dominant in its market that it virtually ignored the existence of competition. Its limited market understanding and reluctance to acknowledge the potential impact of technological development landed it in a position from which it was extremely fortunate to extricate itself – by use of the very disciplines it had earlier ignored. It had allowed Duracell to develop unopposed. Only when it took the trouble to understand the market, and what its competitor was doing, did it develop the strategy which enabled it to regain the market initiative it should never have lost.

Abbey National sized up its building society competition in the 1970s and appeared not to rate it very highly, as it moved into the maverick position in the movement. This judgement and the competitors' lack of response in the early stages allowed Abbey National under Clive Thornton to create a strong, innovative image which made it stand out from the other, traditionally less enterprising societies. The further development into strategic and business-planning disciplines under Peter Birch has been a deliberate move to prepare for the new market conditions and the much more aggressive competition the company will face in 1987.

TSB had also researched the strengths and weaknesses of its future competitors and has developed its strategy to provide meaningful added-value services. Aware that it was not just in competition with clearing banks but with building societies, insurance companies, foreign banks and 'anyone who offers financial services to the personal, professional and commercial markets', it reacted by creating a technology barrier, through heavy investment in automated services and by reaching into those competitors' markets before they could spread into TSB's own.

It is interesting that these two organizations, which developed in a very controlled and orderly environment, should be so much more aware of market and competitive conditions than many manufacturing companies from much tougher stables.

All the companies in the study were very aware of their direct competitors, and most had researched the extent and changing nature of indirect competition. They also accepted fully that the moves they made would inevitably attract competitor response in some form, and most had prepared contingency counter action. Yet again, these companies demonstrated their understanding of another critical factor to achieving success in highly competitive markets.

Crunch highlights

Companies tend to underestimate the competition's action and reaction.

Companies must understand indirect as well as direct competition, and what business they are really in.

Deep understanding of the competition has to be linked to similar understanding of customers.

Competitive advantage

The competitive edge is the core of effective marketing. It determines the competitive advantages which will differentiate the company's product or service from those of competitors and will create a customer preference. The advantage may be higher performance, better design, superior quality, more reliable service back-up, better distribution outlets – anything that satisfies the customer's needs more closely.

As with market segmentation and competition the only way for a company to determine an appropriate advantage is research to understand the market situation, what customers' needs are and what competitors are doing to satisfy those needs.

Creating a consumer preference normally brings a higher perceived value to the product. That in turn permits the supplier to charge higher prices and obtain better margins than would otherwise have been possible. Some advantages, based on an intrinsic product superiority, can be maintained over long periods. However, all too many can be nullified by a competitor matching or undercutting what is on offer.

The price route is normally associated with commodity-type products or services, which to all intents are similar if not identical. If such a commodity product situation is linked to a declining market it is a recipe for price-cutting disaster as has happened over recent years in chemicals and, even more recently, in computers and computer components.

The plain fact is that in the majority of cases competing solely on price is a losers' game. Two pieces of evidence are relevant here. One is Gallup research, which finds that most people will pay more for what they perceive to be quality products.

The other evidence comes from PIMS, which found that companies competing on price have a much lower return on investment than those competing on brand appeal. PIMS does not deny that low costs present a strong barrier against competitors. It does, however, argue against the traditional wisdom on getting there. Continual

114

cost-cutting reduces margins and leads all too easily to cuts that harm customer goodwill. Buying market share is no recipe for creating brand loyalty. By contrast, a focus on quality or another added value feature creates a committed customer base, which can be expanded by degrees. With this expansion comes increased market share and, as a result, lower costs from increased volume. This combination is far more difficult for a competitor, of whatever size or resources, to break. Indeed, to do so he will normally need to follow the same track of quality himself over a period of years.

A third piece of evidence, albeit highly selective, comes from the airline industry, where a number of new competitors have attempted to seize market share by concentrating on price. Two of these – Laker and People's Express – have collapsed and sold up respectively. Whether the retaliation of the major airlines against Laker was fair or unfair, their reaction was inevitable. As they organized resources to meet the price challenge, margins declined all round. But Laker, competing only on price, had no other ties with its customers. Those competitors who held off the challenge had built up reputations for customer service and were thus able to hold on to the vital frequent travellers, who were not prepared to travel in discomfort for one-off price savings. With their larger market share they were able to last the course. Laker didn't.

People's Express grew rapidly to number five in the ranks of US airlines. Again, it took time for the quality airlines to respond with similarly low fare structures. People's Express swiftly gained the nickname 'People Distress', because the low margins it earned on each flight inevitably resulted in complaints of poor service, delays and overbooking. When the majors retaliated its only defence was to slash prices by another 30% – the desperate ploy of a loser. Although the bookings kept coming in it simply did not have the resources to fight a prolonged price war.

It remains to be seen how well the other new airlines, seeking to achieve competitive edge through price, will survive. One argument says that they have recognized the reality that airline tickets are already a commodity. Yet the experience of British Caledonian and British Airways suggests that is not necessarily the case. For long-term survival and growth, companies such as Virgin Atlantic may need to add ingredients other than price to their competitive edge – and to accept that a compromise on lowest costs is necessary.

The other extreme to the commodity product competing on price is the new product meeting a latent or incipient need, where a unique advantage exists in a fast-growing market. This is the ideal situation for high-margin business, but even here the competitive edge must be continually strengthened as rival products try to catch up.

The differential philosophy was basic to the thinking of all the companies studied. In the case of Smith's rebirth in the crisp market, bringing back the original little blue salt packet provided a differential over the competition in a consumer environment, where interest in healthy eating had started to influence attitudes towards salt and ready-salted foods. Smith's blue salt packet was almost a part of the British heritage and its return combined nostalgia with up-to-date health considerations. The surprise was that competitors let Smith's get away with the move without a me-too response.

Bird's Eye exemplifies the opposite position. Its competitive advantage through the Unilever distribution system was destroyed by the arrival of freezer stores, which had a superior location advantage and gave competing frozen food manufacturers a ready outlet.

British Caledonian searched for its competitive edge against the much larger, and equally or better-equipped national airlines, and found little meaningful differential in basic customer service for its business-market segment. It therefore created an easily recognizable advantage in its very efficient and tartan-uniformed Caledonian Girls, and promoted this feature with remarkable success.

BA saw its competitive edge as its operational reputation, its people and its route network. Throughout all the vicissitudes of the 1970s it never cut the level of investment in pilot training. To create an edge with the rest of its people it conducted one of the most extensive training operations ever carried out outside the armed forces – a vast investment for any competitor to match. And it has kept intact most of its route network – in particular, its fifteen destinations in the United States.

Cadbury developed its Wispa bar originally as its answer to Rowntree's Aero, but finished up with a product which was quite different from Aero and distinctive in its own right. Clever advertising reinforced its 'unique' taste and it has now been successfully established as a distinct product. Rowntree had earlier achieved equally impressive success with Yorkie bar, based primarily on its chunky shape, and again supported by distinctive association advertising. In the chocolate and confectionery business there are a number of such successful differentiations, like Aero, Crunchie, Mars, Polo and Flake.

The differential in these products is clear, but in washing powders and detergents it is much more difficult. Hence the strong development of marketing in the companies involved and their very high promotional spending to try to create a perceived advantage for particular brands. A similar situation applies in other food products like sugar, salt, milk and cream, where attempts at establishing differentials have been less successful and the products are still virtual commodities.

In the UK dairy industry, with its almost unique door-to-door daily delivery, the glass bottle has successfully maintained its differential advantage over plastic and cartons, which have tried hard to break its hold on the market. The glass industry researched consumer attitudes and packaging preferences, and identified its preferred status on hygiene, convenience and familiarity grounds. With milk bottlers and distributors its lower cost as a multi-trip container helped to maintain economies of the doorstep delivery system against the less convenient supermarket purchase. To maintain its cost-competitive edge the bottle manufacturers were among the first to use computer-aided design and manufacturing techniques, to produce lighter-weight, lower-cost versions, tailor-made for dairy distribution.

Beecham demonstrated considerable expertise in finding distinctive advantages for its products, based on a cultural talent for finding particular market segments or niches into which it stretched existing brands by changing the pack, the product formulation or the customer appeal. There are many examples of Beecham's success in this approach, and the repositioning of Lucozade as an energy drink for athletes in small, ready-to-use, convenience bottles was a particularly good one. It has carried out a similar exercise with Silvikrin, where the strength of the brand was piggy-backed on to hairsprays and dressings. In toothpaste, Beecham identified a sensitive gum segment and developed a product which matched the special needs of sufferers.

Johnson & Johnson has managed to develop a remarkably strong brand image in the market for baby products. J&J products are perceived by mothers as being specially formulated and the best available for babies, and this perception is supported by its care-oriented, but not apparently aggressive, promotional campaign. Brand strength in the baby market was used as a launching board as the company targeted on the women's skin-care market, where it used a similar appeal to gentleness. The company is now trying to extend this approach to the forty-plus women's market, with suitable special-benefit, distinctive products. Its moves are all the result of deliberate, careful analysis of particular market segments and niches, supported by sharply targeted product development.

Clark's took its large share of the children's shoe market by means of a distinctive edge based on foot health. The company's emphasis on the need for special fitting checks, to avoid possible foot trouble in later life, had a strong appeal to parents naturally concerned to avoid such problems for their children – almost to the extent of inducing guilt feelings if they purchased cheaper alternatives. However, as the birth rate steadily declined Clark's needed to move higher up the age range. It has now moved strongly into the teenage market where it is trying to build an equivalent competitive edge with products custom-developed to meet teenagers' special wants under the 'Levi's for feet' banner.

It is noticeably in these last two examples that the brand image built up is not confined to a specific product or groups of products. In both cases it is the company name that has become associated with caring and quality. In the end, establishing a *corporate* brand, which may last for tens of years, may be far more important than establishing a product brand which may not last a whole decade. However, the corporate brand is itself vulnerable to skilful segmenting by competitors.

Hi-Tec has taken a different approach to finding its advantage. It has identified its sports shoes with champions in particular sports and particularly with figures from the increasingly popular squash, while at the same time creating a distinctive style and design theme in its products.

It also looked for a competitive edge in distribution and found it in the perpetual problem of small retailers – being out of stock. The answer, Hi-Tec decided, was to appoint secondary distributors in the major conurbations. Their job would be to ensure that the small retailers were kept topped up. It took the major competing brands four years to catch up – by which time Hi-Tec had reinforced its hold on the market.

In the advertising business, where creativity and differentiation should be second nature, the cobbler syndrome is much in evidence. There is a remarkable lack of significant competitive difference between most agencies. Saatchi & Saatchi has tried very hard to create its differential brand advantage through its ambitious claims that its client understanding and creativity can produce measurably more cost-effective commercials than its competitors, and by its very basic business-generating approach to advertising. It also claims increasingly to be able to provide a unique range of services arising from recent acquisitions, which range through PR, market research, personnel selection, salary services and management consultancy.

Ogilvy & Mather has a similar approach but uses its client strategy blueprint package supported by the Ogilvy orchestration of client services to create its distinctive edge, which it believes is to serve its clients more effectively than other agencies.

In the highly competitive car-hire market, Hertz has gone for a rifle-shot segmentation approach, with tailor-made packages aimed to provide an edge in its Business Class and American visitor segments. Avis, on the other hand, while holding its own in providing special packages for these segments, has also gone strongly along the technology route, on the basis that with one vehicle much like another, there is little brand loyalty in the business. Ease of computerized booking and return operations is seen as a meaningful benefit on which Avis can major to its advantage, just as its parent has in the US. The major investment in technology represents a financial and time barrier against me-too competitors.

BMW is a company which has created a differential advantage for its products based on no one tangible element. Its competitive edge is multi-faceted without having any special feature. Quality, reliability, efficiency and economy are all projected in the almost matter-of-fact, assumed manner of someone who knows he has something special. Driving a BMW is fun and the driver is portrayed as someone different from the normal run of the mill. BMW works hard to maintain this cult appeal. It is also extremely difficult for a competitor to match. If BMW were to lose that edge it would almost certainly be a result of its own actions rather than those of a competitor.

Another European luxury car maker, Porsche, has founded its

competitive advantage on an exceptional level of customer service. The main bottleneck in its production process is the paintshop. Why? Because Porsche owners have very individual tastes and want individual colours. In some cases, customers have sent in their favourite lipstick for the paintshop to match exactly. The special feeling of being part of the Porsche club has created almost fanatical devotion to the brand. A high proportion of US buyers turn the delivery of their new Porsche into a festive occasion by travelling to Stuttgart to collect it, even though it could be delivered to their door.

Establishing an 'unfair advantage' is part of the corporate culture of 3M. Its emphasis on innovation is aimed at achieving that specific competitive edge. The much higher than normal investment in research and the encouragement of entrepreneurial thinking inevitably produce a stream of new products which the system sifts out before heavy individual funding is required. Since these developments are normally technology based, and ahead in time of the competition, 3M frequently launches unique products into well-researched and understood markets. That has to be a very desirable situation. However, the company has also been creative in its thinking about products such as video tape, which are virtual commodities. Here it gave itself the quality edge it wanted by a lifetime guarantee.

The heavy technical content of Lansing products could have been expected to make for competitive advantage. In reality, however, competitors have little more difficulty matching technological advantages in this area than consumer market companies do in matching design or product formulation advantages. Lansing has concentrated its edge on what it terms its 'Total Involvement' with customers through technical advice, training and service. JCB's competitive environment is similarly tough. Its special edge is simply the intensity of its understanding of its market, its customers and its products and the sheer professionalism of its marketing and management operations.

TSB attempts to fix a competitive edge in four primary areas – price, service, technology and innovation. This is an ambitious goal, but by and large it has succeeded in all four areas, although it has not always been able to hold on to the lead gained. Free banking provided a price edge for a period (long enough to increase its customer base at the majors' expense). The decision to improve service by having longer opening hours six days a week was brave, given the costs involved. But those costs have deterred competitors who would have to spend far more to match the level of convenience. Strategic investment in technology has increased customer service in a number of ways (for example, by providing on-line, up-to-date bank statements) which are difficult to follow without heavy investment. Innovation we will explore in the next section.

Abbey National, too, has sought competitive edge on a broad front. It also has an eye for advantage in consumer service. It was the first building society, for example, to abolish a major irritation for house-buyers – the refusal by the societies to show the results of property surveys. The logic for not doing so was impeccable: the surveys are intended to indicate value from the building society's point of view (i.e. can it get its money back if it has to foreclose?) rather than from the houseviewer's. Abbey recognized that there was a substantial edge to be gained in terms of favourable market positioning as the society that was prepared to take the housebuyer's needs into account. Now most societies have followed suit.

The other building societies have been less easily able to follow Abbey's 'Chequesave' service, however. Assessing its strengths against its competitors' weaknesses, Abbey determined that the ability to handle cheques lay in having such a highly efficient admin-istration system that it could afford to pay interest on current accounts. Over a period of time it invested in upgrading its systems until the difference in efficiency was so great that its competitors could not economically follow suit without at least an equal invest-ment of time and money.

As expected, the particular competitive edge which companies develop varies considerably. But the determination to establish an edge and make it effective was universal, and clearly fundamental to their success. Equally importantly, these companies recognized that they were in a constantly changing competitive environment where an edge could be nullified by an aggressively imaginative competitor. They were therefore concerned to develop and strengthen their competitive advantage by, for example, continued technical develop-ment or research into new ways of improving customer service. These potential advantages may sit on the shelf until needed to fend off a market invader, or be used pre-emptively to build up a near-impregnable barrier.

Crunch highlights

The competitive edge is the core of effective marketing.

The advantage needs to be *meaningful* to the particular market segment.

Identifying or developing a competitive edge requires deep understanding of customers and competitors.

Open-minded perspective

In every activity there are people whose minds are open to the changing environment. They have a sensitivity to what is happening and their initiative or response is usually imaginative. They are not blinkered in their thinking, and often see a situation from a quite different perspective. This special flair or style of open-mindedness was strongly evident in the companies we studied, and it took two forms. The first was their readiness to accept the changing market environment and the second was the creative nature of their reaction.

It reflected a significant change from the robotic style of marketing, and indeed of total management, that was particularly apparent in fast-moving consumer-goods companies in the 1960s and some of the 1970s, when business growth was strong. Organizations became stereotyped; markets were over-researched; new products were tested to excess; advertising, merchandising and selling became systematized.

In that period of growth little damage was done and many companies were successful despite some of their marketing activities rather than because of them. However, as the repercussions of the oil-price hikes spread in the mid 1970s, as demand declined and competition increased, some of the chickens came home to roost. Many marketing people and their philosophies were found wanting.

The mechanical, over-systematized approach to marketing planning and implementation did not produce the bottom-line results expected. Gradually understanding started to replace straight quantitative analysis of research data. Innovative risk-taking and entrepreneurial attitudes began to be used to achieve an edge over competitors. Advertising became much more imaginative and salesmen started to use real selling skills. Competition had forced companies back to creative marketing. While these new attitudes also spread to industrial, service and retail business, in most sectors it was limited to the more enlightened organizations. Most of the companies in the study were in that category and it was refreshing to find how successful they had been.

The TSB did not rest on its very successful laurels and wait idly for privatization. It projected forward to the likely competitive situation in financial services over the following decade, researched attitudes of customers and staff, and started to bring about the culture change the organization needed if it were to cope with the new, highly competitive financial-services environment. Old values and traditional loyalties were carefully blended with new technology and innovative market moves, to widen the base of the business.

Abbey National began to demonstrate its off-beat style in the late 1970s when its entrepreneurial general manager led it along a distinctly maverick route and broke ranks with the very conservative building society movement. What was essentially a stubborn resistance to meekly following the unimaginative majority view of the movement's council on interest rates and lending rules was cleverly projected as trend-setting innovation. In the 1980s Abbey has the much sounder base of clearly defined marketing strategies and disciplines on which to develop its creative approach to the fast-changing financial-services business.

British Airways changed in less than three years from a strongly entrenched, operations-driven, inflexible organization to one dedicated to understanding and satisfying its customers. As with the TSB, this required a culture change and the imaginative implementation of reorientation training programmes based on careful interpretation of extensive research into customer and staff attitudes. British Caledonian considered it had no option but to go down the route of creating a distinctive approach to its customers. With far less muscle than its main competitors, it had to use to maximum effect what little advantage it had. The Caledonian Girls did just that.

For Bird's Eye the trauma of being caught napping triggered what was almost an over-reaction as its whole approach to the business was rethought. The outcome was much more typical of its parent, Unilever; with the development of a carefully researched marketing strategy, rifle replaced shotgun, while creative product development and customer orientation became the basis of a new market-driven company culture.

Smith's market domination was carved up by a combination of aggressive competition, aided by a lack of market awareness on its own part. Regaining its position required a virtual start from scratch in understanding market influences, customer attitudes and preferences on products, and competitors' strengths and weaknesses. With Nabisco resources to support it such a massive research programme could have been done to death in compensation for the previous dearth of information. The new approach did not allow this to happen and research was targeted to support innovation and the creation of competitive advantages. Open-minded realism prevailed even in the extreme peril Smith's found itself in, when many companies in a similar situation would have taken the low-risk, safe route.

Cadbury Schweppes appears to have lost some of the former creativity of the individual companies from which it was formed. Its future success (and possibly independence) will depend on how successful it is in building on the imaginative approach shown with Wispa. Schweppes has shown flashes of creative marketing but nothing on the scale of its packaging innovations of the 1960s. However, there is no doubt that the organization is demonstrating its freedom from the blinkers which were restricting its vision.

Rowntree acknowledged many years ago that its competitive challenge to Cadbury would have to be on imaginative product development and promotion. Its basic belief that it is in the business of providing pleasure, romance and other emotional satisfactions requires it to be creative. It has managed to establish this belief as an integral part of the company philosophy, and has created an organization structure to support it with major emphasis on new-product and concept development.

Beecham has developed over the years a talent for creative market segmentation and brand stretching which is matched by few of its competitors. Its culture and organization are structured to support innovative product development and niche marketing. The Beecham internal environment is a demanding one but it appears to stimulate open minds or perhaps it attracts people with that type of natural talent. Certainly, brands which were withering elsewhere have blossomed with the much more imaginative Beecham treatment.

Johnson & Johnson has its own distinctive brand of freshness and it pervades its whole organization. Its research is aimed at total knowledge of its key markets; competitors are similarly diagnosed, a necessary exercise to achieve the goal of market leadership. The development of special-benefit products is an essential element in this success and, to force new products through, the product champion approach is used. This entrepreneurial talent is encouraged by a remuneration system which rewards it. The other side of this special-benefit coin is the identification of interesting market segments or niches to exploit, and in this J&J take a deliberate, almost clinical approach which is appropriate to their business. Nothing is flamboyant in the approach, which is designed to be in tune with the corporate credo and the markets the company serves. It has also developed a talent for keeping out competitors once it has entered a market segment, without the usual aggressive battling normally associated with the activity. J&J simply takes such a strong position in the market that it is extremely difficult for competitors to make headway. Its very simplicity is its strength. It merely does what is necessary to hold a particular market – by being better than its competitors.

C.&J. Clark is a very deceptive company. It gives the impression of a provincial family organization, yet it operates at a very sophisticated level, particularly in its understanding of its markets, its customers and its competitors. In a low-key way it has identified what really matters in the footwear business – the underlying critical influences, not simply the superficial fashion changes. This understanding is translated into basic trading concepts which separate Clark's from the rest, and it is well illustrated in the very successful approach to children's shoes. The company is also constantly probing new concepts and new technology, to match them to its knowledge of changing market needs and to keep its thinking ahead of competitors'.

Hi-Tec's success is based on its imaginative and pragmatic attitude to its markets. It does what is necessary to gain an edge on its competitors and expand its market, and it has a talent for identifying world trends and translating them into the UK market. Its management style is flexible, and aggressive creativity is critical to its whole operation.

BMW is probably the most creative of the companies in its approach to the market-place. It has developed a very deep understanding of customer motivations and has translated complex engineering and design features into meaningful but often intangible benefits, to match consumers' assessments of what is important to them. BMW has achieved what few companies have done, it has created a tremendous mystique and appeal for its product without the customers really knowing why. There is nothing mechanical in that approach.

Jaguar now has the fundamentals of its business right and as that phase is ending, the company has moved into new imaginative ways of exploiting its re-established reputation, and the strong international appeal of its superb product. The launch of the XJ40 saw the start of this new approach.

Black & Decker operates in the making-life-easier business and it believes it will be successful only if it is better than its competitors – at knowing what influences are impacting on its customers, identifying opportunities and being faster on its feet in exploiting them with suitable products. The essence of its business is imaginative interpretation of a fast-changing environment and Black & Decker has demonstrated its talent at this and at adapting its organization and its approach as necessary.

3M has created the need for innovation and the organization to foster it, by its own objective of having 25% of its business coming from products or services introduced within the previous five years. That can only be achieved in an open-minded corporate environment and 3M has taken this to a level unmatched by many, if any, other companies. It has also managed to superimpose strong planning disciplines on this innovative culture, without any stifling effect, because of the emotional and financial stimulus it gives to creative thinking in all areas of the business.

A strong part of this approach is encouraging people to step outside the routine of their business and to look at it in as many creative ways as possible. Hence its building services and products group, which makes office and factory cleaning systems, posed itself the question: 'As well as concentrating on cleaning up dirt and dust in the building, why don't we help prevent it getting in in the first place?' The question led to the development of a new kind of doormat that allows dirt to drop through the weave and therefore never needs beating.

ICL in the 1970s was not lacking in talent or drive, but its approach was almost *too* dedicated as it went for the straight computer market. In a strong growth market ICL found, as Ever Ready and Smith's did, that companies can survive quite well even with blinkered vision. However, when the market environment changes, freshness in assessing the business situation, and knowing how to exploit it, is essential. These companies are now demonstrating this different approach in their successful recoveries. Others like IBM, JCB and Lansing identified very early in their corporate existence the competitive advantage which stems from open-minded management of their business, and it became part of their culture in both tough and easy market environments.

This open-minded perspective is one of the most significant changes in business thinking over recent years, and to a considerable extent was stimulated by the success of Japanese companies and their different philosophy to marketing strategy. It is also interesting that although manufacturing companies were in greatest need of such a fresh approach, it is most evident in retailing and service businesses.

Crunch highlights

A fast-changing market environment requires an open-minded management and an acceptance of change.

Success requires an imaginative response or initiative to the new situation.

This unblinkered perspective responds to strategic guidelines and is effective in both simple and complex situations.

Marketenvolk

Just as customers make the business, people make the company. It was apparent that, both in the companies studied and in other successful organizations, finding the type of people who performed well in their particular environments was critical. Although they had many ways of achieving a cultural fit, the objective was the same.

In financial services, the business environment had gone through a quite dramatic change and the talents necessary to succeed were quite different from those of the traditional banking operations. The TSB overcame this partially by bringing in new management but mainly by retraining the existing team and changing attitudes. Management and staff understood the need for adapting to the new situation and responded positively to the challenge. Abbey National had a reputation for innovation in the building society movement, and as a result tended to attract its own type of people. To ensure it got them, it built in, as an integral part of its business-planning system, the careful selection of staff and their development through tailor-made training. Performance-related rewards, linked to clearly defined objectives, ensure that, having attracted the right calibre of people, the company motivates them well.

Stephen Davis's study of excellence in banking also found that among the most successful banks the foremost 'soft' value in the corporation was the quality of the people. The best banks spend a great deal of time on personal career planning and careful selection to ensure that they have the right kind of person in the right job. By and large they also 'grow' their own people, on the grounds that outsiders take time to absorb culture and values – and indeed may never do so. Neither TSB nor Abbey National has yet reached the level of confidence in its approach to people that Citibank claims for itself – hire 'as many overachievers as possible, with an inordinate amount of energy; then raise them high'.

In British Airways the change from an operations-driven to a market-driven organization necessitated a fundamental attitude reorientation, which in turn required a massive communications exercise and training programme. 'Putting People First' was aimed at both objectives, demonstrating the interdependence of different groups of employees and focusing attention on the critical importance of the customer and meeting his or her needs. More than twenty thousand employees with direct customer contact have been through this programme. Staff who do not have direct customer contact have undergone similar programmes, emphasizing the need to provide support for those staff who do deal with customers. Research indicates that the reorientation programmes are having the desired effect, and that customers perceive the improved service and positive attitudes on the ground and in flight.

British Caledonian has not had to change employees to a customer-oriented style, but it has had to work hard to maintain it. It does so through careful selection and continuous training to ensure that what the company preaches is also practised to the full.

Saatchi & Saatchi's aim of being the biggest, most profitable and creatively effective agency in the business demands total commitment and high performance from staff. The agency believes that the appeal of such a working environment attracts the 'winners' it needs to achieve its objectives. In other words, the more challenging the job, the better people it attracts. Ogilvy & Mather is equally committed to having high-performance staff, but it has a strong tradition of emphasis on careful selection of young people and developing them through extensive training and communication programmes. Imaginative attitudes to rewarding performance are considered an important feature in the creation of a company environment, which stimulates competitive innovation. As we showed in the first section of this study, the agency is clear that the type of person it wants

is motivated by the demands of excellence
understands balanced judgement and decision-making
has mental agility rather than depth of intellect
has emotional self-confidence
has the ability to communicate.

Compare that profile with that of Hertz's ideal employee, who

has pride in doing the job well
has a strong recovery rate from all the pressures
is a self-starter, aware of opportunities

believes attention to detail is important
understands that a customer's most recent experience is critical.

As in other aspects of the business, each company has identified what is necessary and appropriate to its particular situation.

Hertz aims to attract people who match these requirements by the public image it projects, and then reinforces the characteristics it values through training programmes, aimed primarily at making staff aware of how much their behaviour influences customers and what they need to do to beat their competitors. Again, remuneration is linked to performance and supported by award programmes.

Avis's aggressive attitude to achieving results and beating the competition is drummed into staff through intensive training. The company seeks to hire and develop people who are highly motivated, who identify strongly with the company and its goals. It motivates them at least in part by above-industry levels of remuneration and personal awards. Says Geoff Corbett:

> We recruit the kind of people who will best be able to work in a quality company. Not everyone has the qualities we look for. Our kind of person has a mature outlook (even if he or she is young), customer awareness, and sensitivity. Perhaps most important, they are the kind of people who enjoy and are stimulated by providing a high-quality of service. Sometimes I wish there were more of them. Then I look at how many such people we have and how few there are out there. As long as we can attract them – and having a reputation for being a quality company is one of the major reasons we do attract them – then the edge it gives us over other companies makes me pleased that such talented people *are* so few and far between.

Perhaps not surprisingly when a company rests on its laurels or loses its way, the symptoms show in many areas of the business. There was little evidence of any distinctive Bird's Eye person having been cultivated, until the company started to put its new act together in 1981 to meet the changed market environment. There still is not a distinct set of winning attitudes and activities among the staff, but the company is clearly making great efforts to establish one. It has increased communication and training programmes to ensure that everyone in the organization knows what the corporate objectives are, and to start creating an environment where high performance is not only necessary but expected. The natural next step is to relate rewards to performance. Other developments will no doubt materialize as the new culture is established.

Smith's position is not dissimilar. A major part of the dramatic change in company culture taking place has been the identification of the kind of manager needed in this business environment:

someone who gets things done within a predetermined strategy
is a doer rather than a conceptualizer
is highly accountable
committed to achieving objectives
responds to performance-related remuneration packages.

The characteristics previously required of a Smith's manager were not defined in any specific terms. This same lack of definition is frequently seen in unsuccessful organizations. Smith's considers its training is still unsatisfactory and is taking action to improve it.

Cadbury, like other old-established companies, had a policy on selection and training of people which was considered appropriate to the overall needs of the business and its likely environment. That environment was seen as one of stable, reliable growth. The rigours of the last few years and the potential threat of being taken over were certainly not part of the corporate vision. Cadbury Schweppes is now moving fast to adapt to the new environment and has stated clearly its objectives and what it is doing to achieve them. Creating new attitudes and commitments is a critical part of this change. The question is whether it can be done fast and effectively enough to escape possible predators. Certainly the company is bringing in and promoting strong, aggressive management in an attempt to do so.

Rowntree has a long tradition and reputation for being interested in its people, going back to Seebohm Rowntree, and it has modified and updated its selection and development thinking as the needs of the business changed. The present typical Rowntree person is claimed to be:

ambitious, with a strong desire to succeed
ready to be judged on performance.

Beecham has developed a unique culture, which places great emphasis on achieving planned objectives in its various businesses, and it is strongly market driven. As a direct result, it demands high performance from a relatively small number of people who influence what happens in the company and its markets. It also encourages calculated risk-taking and fast action. Such an environment calls for a particular kind of marketing person who has been referred to variously as:

creative and streetwise
an intelligent barrow boy.

Beecham focuses its training on the basic fundamentals of the business. Most learning comes on the job, which brings through a particular type of talent appropriate to the environment which bred it. Since the organization tends to be managed by people who have developed primarily through the marketing function, this culture is continuously reinforced. Johnson & Johnson also has a very individual business style, but it is quite different from Beecham's. Because its approach to its markets is one of leadership from special benefit products, it encourages and rewards entrepreneurial talent. The J&J person is seen as:

well educated
ambitious
having strong personal values.

J&J does not see training as a centralized activity but rather as the managers' responsibility. Against the background of the all-pervading credo, this responsibility is taken seriously, as is the need to have a strongly motivated staff.

The prime driving force at Black & Decker is identifying opportunities and matching products to them. At 3M it is essentially the same although oriented more heavily towards innovative technical research. In both companies this requires people who respond to this type of environment, and it also stimulates a strong market awareness in the technical R&D areas. The extent to which both companies have achieved success reflects the effectiveness of their selection and training. Although neither company specifies a particular type of ideal person, they clearly manage to find them. They have also placed considerable importance on communicating their philosophies throughout their organizations. In particular, they make sure everyone understands the critical necessity for such a heavy investment in innovative thinking, to produce market-place results by finding new and better ways of doing things.

In 3M this philosophy goes back a long way. More than forty years ago William L. McKnight, who did more than any other man to shape 3M, told his managers:

> As our business grows, it becomes increasingly necessary to delegate responsibility and to encourage men and women to exercise their initiative. Those men and women to whom we delegate authority and responsibility, if they are good people, are going to want to do the jobs in their own way.
>
> Mistakes will be made. But if a person is essentially right, the mistakes are not as serious in the long run as the mistakes management will make, if it undertakes to tell those under its authority exactly how they must do their jobs. Management that is destructively critical when mistakes are made, kills initiative. And it is essential that we have many people with initiative if we are to grow.

That well-worn statement 'people are our greatest asset' has been a matter of practical reality at IBM since the foundation of the organization by Thomas J. Watson. IBM looks for self-starters who can communicate and it develops such talents through regular training and career moves. It considers training and manpower planning as critical to the success of the company, and its employees are expected to spend 5% of their time on training activities. Since it places such importance on customer service and excellence in all its activities, special attention is given to the selection, development and motivation of the people who will provide it.

Following the reassessment of the total ICL operation, new people came in with clearly defined objectives of what was necessary to change the company. Having the right organization structure and people in place quickly was essential. An audit indicated that much talent was already there, but attitudes and orientation needed changing. To achieve the change, several million pounds were invested in a huge executive retraining programme, which included board members. The commitment to it went from top to bottom of the organization.

The philosophy and practice in the companies varied in specific features, but there was a common core running through them all:

Identifying what constituted a performer.
Placing these people in key positions.
Training and developing them.

Demanding high performance.

Motivating and rewarding them in the most appropriate way.

In all cases having the right people for the particular company and its environment was considered critical, as was having the right training and motivation to make them high-level performers.

ICI is another company which has put its house in order and is driving hard in its chosen markets. In a recent interview Denys Henderson, the new chairman, said, 'We have always had an emphasis on high-quality people, with a personnel policy that is human but realistic. Without the right people, the rest would crumble.'

Crunch highlights

Although they called them by different names, all the companies were looking for 'performers'.

Such people respond to clearly defined objectives.

The type of training and motivation depends on the individual and the company environment, but is invariably based upon giving performers the scope to perform.

Dedication

In many companies the most common goal is what is termed the budget, and often it is the only goal. The budget is the financial implication of what is expected to happen in the market-place and in the internal operations of the company. It is in most cases what the company hopes to achieve, rather than a commitment to achieve.

In a minority of companies, longer-term strategic plans are prepared. These are developed after an examination of the likely economic, political, social and business environment in which the company will be operating over the following three, five or ten years depending on the nature of the business. The strategic plan also establishes the key market, development and financial objectives and the strategic focus for achieving them.

Companies with this degree of sophistication would normally have an annual business or operating plan which spells out the specific objectives for each part of the business and the financial outcome of achieving them. This business plan is developed from the bottom up to meet the overall objectives of the business, and as people participate in its development they also identify with the objectives and the need to achieve them.

In a recent study of Japanese subsidiaries in the UK, and matched British companies, this participation in the development of strategies and operating plans was common to the former and virtually nonexistent in the latter. Since it is almost a truism that people feel much more committed to something they have participated in preparing, it is not surprising, if the study was anything like typical, that management and staff in Japanese companies are much more dedicated to achieving their objectives than those in British companies, where the goals have been thrust upon them.

Most of the companies in our study had strategic plans. All of them had business plans with clearly defined objectives which in most cases had been developed from well down the organization, and had been widely communicated to ensure that the reasons for the objectives, and the importance of being committed to achieving them, were understood.

Participating in the planning process creates involved attitudes and although these can be strong, the evidence from the study indicated that dedication to the achievement of the business objectives required emotional and material motivation, and success-linked rewards. It also required that people were clear on what was expected of them and properly trained to achieve it. To maximize commitment also required an understanding of the people involved and of their driving forces.

The environment and the level of dedication did vary of course, not just between companies but between divisions of the same company. This is to be expected and it was noticeable that the level of commitment tended to parallel the strength of the organization's marketing credo. In the TSB, for example, management and staff knew what they were expected to achieve and there was conviction that they would achieve what was asked of them, but this did not appear to have been spelt out to the extent that it had in other companies. Abbey National had gone further towards performance-related remuneration with the clearly defined objectives this requires. This had strengthened the sense of dedication to achieving objectives.

British Airways placed major importance on ensuring that everyone in the organization knew why the company was changing its approach, what the new objectives were and why it was so important that they were achieved. The lengths the executives went to to get the message across were described in an earlier section and the massive communication and training exercise demonstrated the company's conviction. The staff responded to it with an impressive level of commitment and loyalty. In British Caledonian, the need for dedication to being the best airline for business travellers was understood very early in the development of the airline. Originally (and still) necessary for survival, this commitment has now become a matter of pride and conviction, and those are powerful motivations.

The two advertising agencies set out to attract the type of people who are motivated by competition and challenge. When such people identify with a company and its objectives the organization's goals become personal. When the dedication this induces is reinforced by the same commitment from the chairman and senior management, and remuneration is linked to performance, people will make extra-ordinary efforts to achieve remarkable results.

Hertz believes it has developed a similar style of employee, who has a pride in doing the job well, who has a commitment to the company objectives of being aware of customers' wants and pro-viding performance to meet them. The company also believes that its recent strong improvement was due largely to this dedication and to performance-linked rewards. The extensive training programmes and greater responsibility delegated to branches have also strength-ened the sense of dedication.

Avis has an aggressive approach to the achievement of objectives. This is instilled in its staff by training and involvement and is reflec-ted in their attitudes and motivation. It supports this with high remu-neration and incentives. Not surprisingly, its staff identify strongly with the company and are committed to meeting its goals.

The company also ensures that all staff know and understand the company strategy. An annual roadshow by the top management team takes the financial results and plans for next year to employees around the country.

Top management also demonstrates its commitment (and gets close to the customer) through its visible management scheme. Every man-ager, including the chief executive, spends at least one week at the sharp end of the business, washing cars, taking reservations or working on the rental counter. That often means that the executive has to learn how to do these junior jobs. Corbett recalls with glee how, as he fumbled to get used to the reservations terminal, an American visitor asked him: 'Say, sonny, isn't it about time you went back to training school?'

On Corbett's wall hangs a collection of the many prizes and awards the company has won in recent years. Among them is a single picture of a skull and crossbones – a reminder to all of the one year the com-pany didn't win any major awards. Neither Corbett nor any of his executives would countenance the possibility of that shame occurr-ing under their management.

It would be interesting, if it were possible, to compare in detail the relative level of dedication and commitment of managers in com-panies such as Bird's Eye, Smith's, Ever Ready and ICL, who have pulled their organizations out of difficult situations, with those of managers in companies which have been consistently successful, such as IBM, 3M, JCB and Rowntree. Is becoming successful a stronger motivation than remaining successful? Is the psychological make-up of the person or the corporate culture more critical? From the companies studied, it would appear that the answer varies with the environment and particularly with the style of the chief executive.

In Bird's Eye, having reacted to the competitive threat, the company increased its communication and training programmes to ensure that the situation was understood and to stimulate commitment to the action that was necessary to re-establish market leadership. With Smith's the problems were much more serious and the solutions went deeper, with a basic change in the style of management and managers. An essential feature of the new profile was a commitment to achieving objectives and responding to performance-related remuneration.

In companies like Cadbury and Rowntree there has always been a strong commitment among employees. It goes back to the origins of the business, when the caring attitudes of the owners for the welfare of their workers were first expounded. During periods of stable growth and with limited competitive pressures, the traditional style of dedication was adequate, but in the present environment of aggressive competition and financial performance pressures, a much sharper market-oriented commitment is necessary. Cadbury has clearly discovered this and is moving to implement it throughout its management and organization, with much stronger emphasis on customer satisfaction. Chairman Sir Adrian Cadbury underlines this: 'We are in business to meet the needs of consumers internationally for products and services of good value and consistent quality.'

The softer, traditional attitudes, which appear on the surface at Rowntree, conceal a much tougher culture where commitment to performance is an integral part of day-to-day management. As Chairman Kenneth Dixon says, 'We can only continue to satisfy our customers if we can offer competitive products. This is the only sustainable source of prosperity and job security.'

Beecham is at the opposite end of the spectrum. There is no doubt about what it expects from its managers and other employees. They quite simply have to achieve their market-place and financial objectives – the idea that they might not do so is not countenanced – and the two objectives are closely linked in an organization which is strongly market led from the top. Being beaten to the punch by a competitor is considered a devastating blow, probably even more by the particular manager than by the company. Winning or losing is a matter of personal pride and the financial and career effects are strong motivators. Although the dedication to performance is strong, the type of manager such an environment attracts is likely to move on if Beecham is not able to satisfy his career aspirations.

Johnson & Johnson's company credo has a strong influence on attitudes within the organization, and on the type of person in it. There is no lack of conviction that objectives have to be achieved. Quite the contrary. But achieving objectives involves an analytical, almost clinical approach, which could be considered more sophisticated. It is certainly no less effective, as the J&J leadership of its markets demonstrates very clearly. Even the terminology reflects the corporate culture. J&J is careful to refer to market leadership rather than dominance. However, J&J still has a remuneration system that encourages and rewards entrepreneurial, performance-achieving talent.

The Clark's organization has a strong tradition of concern for the wellbeing and development of its people. Associated with this are extensive training programmes and communications exercises to ensure that the company progress and objectives are understood. This involvement philosophy has fostered tremendous loyalty to Clark's and high commitment to ensuring its success.

Hi-Tec has no long-established traditions, but because it is young and developing fast its managers identify themselves strongly with the company goals. This is frequently the case in entrepreneurial businesses. The trick is to maintain the same commitment and enthusiasm as the organization matures. The company operates in a tough business with an American-style approach which emphasizes achievement and links reward to it.

In re-establishing excellence, Jaguar had to involve the whole organization in raising performance standards if the company were to seize back its top place in world markets. In this environment, with new people in key positions and with rapid success it is not surprising that people are enthusiastic and dedicated. Leading the commitment is Chairman Sir John Egan: 'We are all in the business of trying to satisfy customers and it is a task for everyone from the managing director, who gives the customer his home telephone number, to the mechanic who is prepared to turn out at any time to help the customer out.'

Black & Decker has an interesting combination of freedom to innovate, very disciplined marketing and strong financial orientation. Successful new products do not just happen with the regularity that Black & Decker has achieved. They are made to happen, because the people concerned know the company's future growth depends on it and because they will do what is necessary to secure that growth.

3M is structured to achieve the practical creativity which gives the company an edge over the competition, in whatever way is appropriate. It has an unusual culture which emphasizes innovation oriented to the market-place and rewards success in what it considers emotionally satisfying ways, since normal remuneration is high. Losers are also supported and encouraged to be successful next time. This kind of environment is likely to appeal to a special type of person who will thrive on self-motivation. Scarce as such people are, 3M appears to experience no problem in attracting and motivating them. Recently, *Fortune* magazine commented: 'What keeps them satisfied in 3M is the knowledge that anyone who invents a new product, or promotes it when others lose faith, or figures out how to mass produce it economically, has a chance to manage that product as though it were his own business and to do so with a minimum interference from above.'

IBM's attitude to the people it employs is in line with the high standards it applies to all its activities. It demands much of them, gives them the tools to achieve what they are asked, and rewards them well for doing so. A former chief executive officer of IBM once observed that the corporation was prepared to change everything except its basic business beliefs. 'IBM's approach to people is based on respect for the individual. In pursuit of this, the company helps individuals to develop their full potential and make the best use of their abilities. If an individual is given an atmosphere of trust, responsibility, security and encouragement, he will do his best work. High productivity and profits follow.' With such people in such an environment, commitment is not a problem. Many of ICL's people have been to the brink, have now come back and are again part of a successful, enterprising company. That by itself would tend to stimulate dedication to remaining successful; but when combined with a new aggressive and confident style of management, which knows exactly where it is going and how it is going to get there, commitment becomes greatly strengthened.

JCB and Lansing are tough, demanding companies. They have to be to survive against intense international competition. Their people are chosen to match this very rigorous environment and both companies expect high performance, and commitment to the achievement of the corporate objectives, which are communicated clearly and widely throughout both organizations. The emphasis on achievement is supported by performance-related rewards and high technical investment.

The degree of dedication to the achievement of corporate success was impressive – particularly where the companies had undergone extensive manning reductions or management change. One of the results of the last six years of redundancies at all levels in British companies during the late 1970s and early 1980s has been a change in the traditional loyalty and commitment. Research also suggests that people remaining in companies where redundancies have occurred have changed their attitudes and have adopted a much stronger element of self-interest in their views and attitudes. It would appear that the companies in this study have largely managed to overcome that trend by a combination of involvement, motivation and sound management.

Crunch highlights

Dedication is the result of involvement, communication, training and motivation.

It requires an understanding of what motivates particular people in a particular environment.

It needs regular reinforcing from top management.

PART THREE

MARKETING EXCELLENCE DISTILLED

The ten fundamental influences on market success identified in the preceding pages vary in their emphasis from company to company. The size and type of markets, the legacy of past successes and failures, all contribute to the corporate profile. All companies, like all people, are products of their environment. None the less, all of the companies exhibited all of the characteristics.

It is significant that all of these ten characteristics were within the companies' own control. They did not depend on external factors. What these companies had done, others could also do – which makes it all the more surprising that these characteristics are not adopted and implemented more widely.

In the first part of the book we looked at the companies in the context of their individual environments and at the elements which were particularly influential to their individual success. In the second part we identified the common denominators. These could be used as a checklist against which companies could compare their own attitudes and operations. However, all organizations have their special circumstances. It may be more valuable to start with a broader characterization, which we can arrive at by distilling the ten common features identified in Part Two into three fundamental factors, which we call for convenience 'the three Cs':

Culture
Creativity
Commitment.

Corporate culture

The culture of a company is critical to its success or failure. Although this is so basic as to be a truism, it is remarkable how frequently a corporate culture is out of time with the environment in which it is operating. In takeover battles the ultimate outcome is heavily dependent on shareholders' views of whether the culture of the predator is more likely to be effective in the particular competitive environment than that of the victim. Many companies have declined and eventually gone out of business because their culture has not adapted to a new business environment.

The corporate culture is influenced by many factors, but above all by the chief executive. Many companies underestimate the impact of the chief executive. Indeed they seem to go to great lengths to assure that he does not influence the culture. None the less, if the chief executive does not direct the company culture, there will still be one. It will be either indecisive or negative depending on the role the chief executive plays. It is not accidental that most strong, positive, successful companies have chief executives with the same characteristics. Unfortunately, the reverse also applies.

Central to the most successful cultures is the supremacy of the customer and the market environment in which the company operates. In such companies the chief executive directs attention to the basic fact that only if the customer purchases does the company have a business. The individual discipline of the chief executive did not appear to be critical to the formation of this market and customer orientation. Although the majority of chief executives had been heavily involved in marketing operations, others had become aware of the importance of satisfying market needs after careers in finance, manufacturing and other major functional areas.

Against the background of this market orientation the effective company culture was marked by the clarity of its mission and objectives. To be successful it was essential to know precisely where the company was going, what it was aiming to achieve and how. The precise nature of this varied from the Johnson & Johnson credo, the mission statement of IBM, ICL, Cadbury Schweppes, British Airways and Lansing to the less well-expressed but no less transparent strategies and objectives of TSB, Clark's, Duracell, Beecham and JCB.

Also central to these successful corporate cultures was the total acceptance of the need to understand the market environment in which the company was operating and the need to adapt to changes in it. A major reason why so many companies have mediocre or catastrophic performance is that they fail to adapt an originally successful strategy to a changed environment. This is probably a far more common cause than poor strategies to begin with. Understanding the market environment usually requires effort, financial resources and constant vigil. Just how companies collect data will vary and is of less importance than their acceptance that they have no choice but to understand their market environments. Using the information is important to these companies, not the volume of data collected. Often the volume of data and its practical application were in inverse ratio.

The final element in the successful culture was honesty in assessing the company's strengths and weaknesses, and how they compared against those of direct and indirect competitors. In a number of cases in the study, companies had either rested on the laurels of previous success (success that had often been built on three Cs) or had ignored or even been unaware of the changes in their environment. Many companies have continued with products, manufacturing processes or even customers which were becoming obsolescent or obsolete; while competitors had identified or created change and the opportunities that normally accompany it. The examples are plentiful, ranging from steel, textiles, cycles, packaging, radios and watches to a wide variety of services.

The other lesson, which has often been learned too late, is that it takes much less to retain customers than to win them back once they have gone. Many customers are reluctant to move from a supplier with whom they may have been dealing for a considerable time. They delay the change for reasons of loyalty, inertia or lack of conviction for much longer than rational business judgement would suggest. To hold these customers often takes much less effort than the unknown new supplier needs to break in. It can take a remarkable amount of customer disorientation to lose customers – yet many companies seem to be adept at doing so.

The successful corporate culture is an amalgamation of understanding and attitudes. It requires the total involvement and influence of the chief executive in directing the orientation of the company towards the market-place, in focusing attention on the customers and competitors in the market, and on the changes affecting it. The effective culture also requires a clear definition of the real mission of the company, its strategy and specific objectives, and the communication of this information throughout the organization. It involves the honest assessment of the company's positive and negative assets compared with the changing needs of its market environment and what competitors have developed or are developing. And finally, it takes a readiness to make the necessary changes in attitudes, products, technology, facilities, organization, markets, customers and people.

In essence, the successful corporate culture is the one which is fully oriented to *identifying* what needs to be done to be successful in the market and to *doing* what is necessary to achieve it. Doing the right things right.

Creativity

The second fundamental factor was the creativity which companies applied in their approach to their businesses. This was especially apparent in the way they examined the environment in which they were operating. They amassed information on socio-economic changes and gathered market research data to identify opportunities the company could exploit or to alert the organization to the need for change. Unlike so many companies, they did not gather information to support decisions which had effectively already been taken. The successful companies applied creative analysis to the market information, continually seeking new insights into the needs and wants of customers and potential customers. In particular, 3M, Black & Decker, Johnson & Johnson, Beecham, Clark's and Rowntree put enormous effort into examining data to see what latent and incipient opportunities could be identified that would provide the opportunity for launching a new product or service or to steal a lead on competitors. This creative approach to the environment was also applied to the segmentation of markets. They looked well beyond the obvious segments to find the niches where substantial new opportunities were available and where a leadership position could rapidly be acquired.

The other side of this coin is the establishment within the company of a creative attitude to thinking about new products. This had been developed to a high level in many of the companies in the study. The techniques and the emphasis varied considerably, as would be expected, with 3M on the one hand and Black & Decker on the other exemplifying the two extremes of approach. 3M's emphasis is on creativity in research and development of products, which were then linked to needs in the market-place; Black & Decker focuses its creativity on identifying, from economic and life-style research, where new-product opportunities exist and then activating the product-development process to produce them. Beecham takes yet another approach. It majors on identifying how changes in the market environment provide opportunities for stretching their existing brands into new segments, or for modifying existing brands to create new segments or niches, by taking advantage of changes in the market.

The successful companies also applied a great deal of creativity in thinking about their strengths and weaknesses, and how these positive and negative assets could be adapted to maximum advantage. This was a major factor in the turnaround of Ever Ready, which made a realistic but creative assessment of the potential of its zinc manufacturing facilities. Smith's did much the same with its food extrusion capabilities. Too often assets are written off when a more imaginative approach to other ways of using them could avoid an expensive disposal.

Understanding what made their competitors tick is a strong feature of the companies in the study, and they display considerable creativity in the ways in which they find out about competitors and how those competitors are likely to act and react in particular situations. JCB knows the strengths and weaknesses of its international competitors in remarkable detail and uses this information both to anticipate their moves and to hit them where they are most vulnerable. Saatchi & Saatchi and Ogilvy & Mather see creativity as their central strengths, and both agencies apply it not only in campaigns for their clients but in their whole business approach. To them it is a major plank for corporate growth. Both Avis and Hertz acknowledge that, virtually everything having been tried in the rental business, success comes from being more imaginative than competitors in understanding what matters to customers. A similar situation applies in the airline business, where psychological influences play a major role. Interpreting and satisfying those psychological needs in a more meaningful way than the competition is an essential ingredient for success.

Central to successful business is the identification and understanding of customers' needs, and providing an offering to match them. However, when competitors are also providing such products or services, it is essential to provide a reason for customers to prefer yours, and that is where companies like 3M and Black & Decker use their product-innovation talents, BMW its package of emotional appeals, IBM its reputation for service and efficiency, TSB its reputation for caring, British Caledonian its concern for customers, Hi-Tec its design, and Beecham its brand strength. Establishing a meaningful differential in a product or service is essential to avoid competing solely or primarily on price and the business becoming a commodity one. All the companies were very aware of the importance of establishing a competitive edge. In most cases, they had achieved it.

Creativity is normally most in evidence in the presentation of the product; in its design, packaging, promotion and merchandising. In recent years there have been efforts to establish design almost as an end in itself, and in some areas it has been suggested that a well-designed product would sell simply because of its design. In fact, design is only one of a number of essential aspects which influence the success or failure of a product. The others include quality, function, packaging, presentation, price, service, and above all the extent to which it meets the needs of customers. It is usual to associate creativity in the development and presentation of a product with consumer goods, but the industrial and service companies studied also used it extensively. Aesthetic design and ergonomic considerations were very much in evidence in Lansing and JCB, both of which spent a great deal of time considering how the product would appeal to both the purchaser and the user. Both companies used sophisticated presentation techniques to communicate these factors to their customers. Similarly, for both IBM and ICL the design of products and the colours of video screens were the outcome of creative interpretation of extensive research programmes. In TSB and Abbey National the whole attitude to customer communications has undergone fundamental change. In both companies a new creative approach was evident in premises, lay-out, range of product offerings and the way they were presented.

The same fresh, imaginative attitudes are apparent in the way these companies have adapted their organization structures to match the needs of the market and the customers in it. Their orientation is not towards the products or services they produce but to groups of customers and to providing the products and services those customers want. These companies also expended considerable imagination on communications to ensure that everyone understood what was happening and why it was essential to achieve the objectives which had been established. In most cases there were also creative approaches to the methods of remuneration and particularly to some form of performance-related incentives.

Creativity pervaded the whole thinking of the companies in the study. They constantly strove for better and more imaginative ways of doing things. Above all, they looked for creative insights into the environment in which they were operating and the influences affecting it – economic, social, political, technological and competitive – and into producing products and services to match this changing environment and which were better or more suitable than those offered by competitors.

Increasingly, success will depend not on whether or not a company is creative, but on the level of creativity and how much it is an integral part of the corporate culture.

Commitment

The third factor was the attitude of commitment, which applied to all aspects of the business. It begins with the chief executive and permeates the organization until everyone has a clear understanding of the corporate mission, the specific objectives, how they are going to be achieved, and their role in achieving them. Top management has taken considerable trouble to communicate the rationale behind the goals, against the background of the trading environment in which the business was operating, and the political, economic, social and other pressures it was likely to face. It sees communication as a critical prerequisite to commitment, and is prepared to make a major investment of finance and of senior management time to ensure that it is carried out effectively.

The same dedication is evident in the search for meaningful data about the market environment and the emphasis on knowing it better than competitors do, in order to create a competitive advantage for their product or service. Hi-Tec's intention is to be better informed and wider awake than the competition. Beecham's aim is to identify new niches or product extensions, Johnson & Johnson's to find likely areas for the company to establish market leadership. 3M and Black & Decker showed extraordinary devotion to linking new-product developments to market opportunities. British Caledonian put similar effort into gathering data to identify what was necessary to retain the business travellers upon which its market niche is based. TSB and Abbey National needed information to reorientate attitudes and activities within the company. In all cases employees understood why the data collection was essential, and were determined to find what was necessary.

Such was the commitment in many of the companies that they took the possibility of a competitor beating them to the punch as a serious failure, both in terms of a missed opportunity and a blow to personal pride. For companies such as JCB, BMW, Avis, Hertz, British Airways and Beecham, this made knowing the competitors and understanding their behaviour a matter of critical importance.

Most of the companies looked for a particular type of person and some clearly defined the profile. Ogilvy & Mather looked for people with specific motivations. Hertz's strong recovery was based on self-starters who respond well to pressures; 3M looked for innovators, IBM for self-starting communicators, Rowntree for people with a strong desire to succeed, Beecham for intelligent barrow boys and Johnson & Johnson for ambitious people with strong personal values. Deeper probing showed that they were attempting to describe the qualities which brought high performance in their particular environment. Those successful companies with less-defined profiles still look for performers who achieve results because their psychological make-up makes it important to them. These people do not come from one particular background, training or functional discipline. Indeed, they come from a wide variety of personal inclinations and environments. The common factor among them is a strong commitment to succeed and an ability to make things happen.

While these talents are essentially inherent, they can be developed and directed. Many of the companies have training programmes aimed at strengthening and targeting these personal characteristics. All had strongly positive attitudes to training, but options varied on the most effective way of doing it. Approaches range from the highly developed programmes of IBM, ICL, British Airways, Ogilvy & Mather and Clark's to the on-the-job style of Beecham and the individual managerial responsibility at Johnson & Johnson.

Whatever the type of performer they look for, they believe that motivating these people is critical to the success and growth of the business. Motivation takes many forms and is tailored to appeal to the specific needs of the company's particular type of performer. Almost all companies acknowledge that performance-related remuneration packages stimulate the type of people who produce results. The challenge is to find the most effective form of incentives for the particular corporate environment, and to maintain its effectiveness in both buoyant and poor trading circumstances.

These companies have created a culture and management process which involves their people in the understanding and analysis of their market environment, and in the development of objectives and action programmes, and stimulates a conviction that they have to be and will be achieved. Because this commitment starts at the top, permeates the whole organization and is supported by performance-linked remuneration, it is not surprising that it is extremely effective.

The companies in this study demonstrate the critical importance of getting the fundamentals of the business right – understanding the changing market environment and creatively developing the strategy and organization to exploit it.

Too many other companies appear to concentrate attention on how to use the tactics and tools, without determining the strategy within which they should be used. It is not surprising that so many of them have paid the ultimate price.